ARCHITECTURE IS FUN

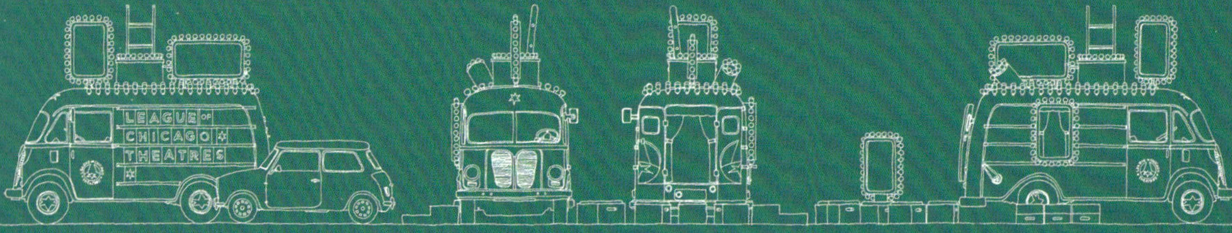
LEAGUE OF
CHICAGO
THEATRES

ARCHITECTURE IS FUN

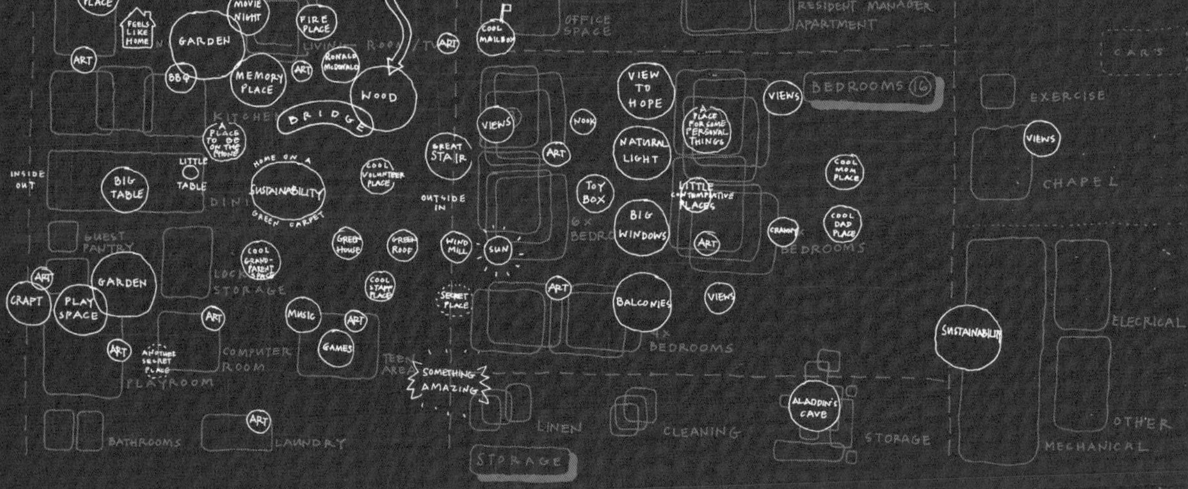
THINGS THAT MAKE YOU GO WOW
SPACES
CONNECTIONS
COMMON SPACE
VIEW FROM HOPE
NICE WALK
STAFF
OTHER
LIBRARY
TURRET
PHOTO PLACE
BLUE VELVET COUCH
FEELS LIKE HOME
MOVIE NIGHT
FIRE PLACE
GARDEN
ART
BBQ
MEMORY PLACE
RONALD McDONALD
LIVING ROOM / TV
WOOD
BRIDGE
KITCHEN
A PLACE TO BE ON THE PHONE
LITTLE TABLE
INSIDE OUT
BIG TABLE
HOME ON A SUSTAINABILITY GREEN CARPET
DINING
COOL VOLUNTEER PLACE
GREAT STAIR
OUTSIDE IN
GUEST PANTRY
COOL GRAND-PARENT SPACE
LOCKER STORAGE
GREEN HOUSE
GREEN ROOF
WIND MILL
SUN
CRAFT
PLAY SPACE
COOL STAFF PLACE
SECRET PLACE
MUSIC
GAMES
ANOTHER SECRET PLACE
COMPUTER ROOM
PLAYROOM
TEEN AREA
SOMETHING AMAZING
BATHROOMS
LAUNDRY
HOUSE MANAGER OFFICE
OFFICE SPACE
COOL MAILBOX
RESIDENT MANAGER APARTMENT
VIEWS
NOOK
VIEW TO HOPE
NATURAL LIGHT
A PLACE FOR SOME PERSONAL THINGS
BEDROOMS (16)
TOY BOX
LITTLE CONTEMPLATIVE PLACES
BIG WINDOWS
6x BEDROOMS
COOL MOM PLACE
COOL DAD PLACE
BEDROOMS
BALCONIES
4x BEDROOMS
LINEN
CLEANING
ALADDIN'S CAVE
STORAGE
CONFERENCE
CARS
EXERCISE
CHAPEL
SUSTAINABILITY
ELECRICAL
OTHER MECHANICAL

CONTENTS

PREFACE

Back in 1994, we wrote an essay entitled *FUN with Sharon and Peter.* It was an elementary way to announce who we were and what we were constructing.

> *Peter is an architect. See Peter draw.*
> *Sharon is an educator. See Sharon teach.*
> *Look what they do together!*

Reminiscent of reading primers, we began championing a *look-say-play* approach. Look at what we can build together. Say what you want and need. Play with us and build a common vocabulary of design. This is how we construct architectural literacy. This is how we share stories. This is how we purposefully make everyday life *fun.*

At work, we are expert children at play. Architecture, design, and experience form our playground where we challenge rules and boundaries. We draw inside and outside of the lines alongside our clients and their communities. We see the power of play as a motivator for engagement, for well-being, and for making a better world.

Play is an invitation to Architecture Is Fun. Through architecture, play can be manifest, challenged, and celebrated. Finding out who will play (and live, work, and learn) in our buildings is an intriguing challenge. We like to discover the architectural stimuli that will give character to a building. Often this involves the universal language of Play. Play fits all bodies. Play is accessible. Play inspires innovation. Play puts us in the present. Play engages us. Play is memorable. Play connects us to others and to the world.

While *Dick and Jane* live in *Anytown*, Architecture Is Fun draws out *unique* responses for each design project to reflect community, culture, and need. To counter some of the overwhelming seriousness in the world, we believe it is more important than ever to play. Dreaming helps to envision a more hospitable, resilient, and happy future.

This primer offers a glimpse into our participatory process and why we believe that architecture and play are transformative.

The evolution for *FUN with Sharon and Peter* is *Architecture Is Fun.* Immediately we saw that as the only way to describe our practice. Having fun is our mantra, our agreement with clients, and our purpose for design.

Our goal is to live up to our name.

Sharon Exley and Peter Exley

ARCHITECTURE,

PUBLIC SPACE, AND PLAY

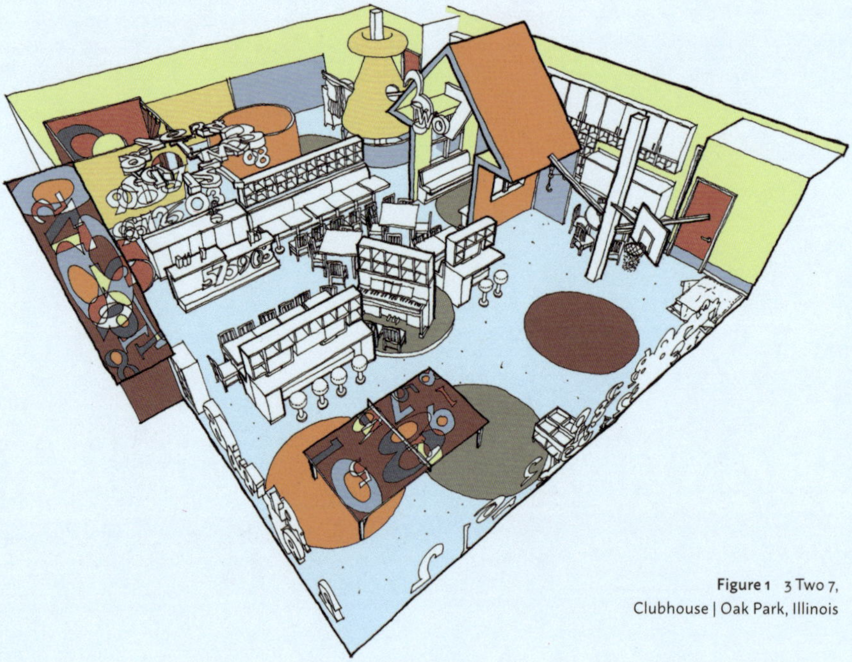

Figure 1 3 Two 7,
Clubhouse | Oak Park, Illinois

Figure 2 Kansas Children's Discovery Center,
Children's Museum | Topeka, Kansas

Figure 3 Children's Museum of Fond du Lac,
Children's Museum | Fond du Lac, Wisconsin

Figure 4 Beanstalk Kids,
Preschool Learning Center | Chicago, Illinois

We make everyday life fun through architecture and experience. We make learning more fun, work more fun, and play even *more* fun. We are also advocates—leading the charge via architecture and design—that play is a basic human right for all, not just for children.

Architecture Is Fun began fortuitously with a design invitation for an exhibit at Chicago Children's Museum, a place we frequented as a family. For many children, our PlayMaze exhibit is the very first museum experience of their lives [see figure 5]. It nurtures curiosity and empathy through urban role-play, turning inquisitive toddlers into interested and interesting citizens, and has done so successfully for over twenty years. Its longevity demonstrates its positive ripple effect on early childhood education, with over 400,000 children and their families visiting every year. Doing that for so many children carries a social purpose that goes beyond bright colors and appropriately scaled furnishings.

Figure 5 PlayMaze, Chicago Children's Museum | Chicago, Illinois

The purpose of PlayMaze, and places like it, is to train citizens to become more inquisitive and empathetic, in the hope they will contribute to the greater good.

PlayMaze had a profound effect on the direction and diligence of our engagement in the development of every subsequent project. Then and now, we accept collaboration as a challenge. Inviting everyone to the design table results in a plurality of thought alongside our deep dives into research, mission, and pedagogies, all of which enriches our architecture, builds play, and constructs consensus.

To demystify the design process and make it accessible, we link architecture and story. We create narratives and illustrations that anticipate desired outcomes, embed values, and underscore play and learning. We learned early on that sharing the story of a place is just as important as what it might look like, what it might contain, and how it might function (what architects prosaically refer to as the program or brief). Our design process uses storytelling to articulate the big picture—the meaning and outcomes people and communities desire and deserve. These are the experiences, events, and emotive qualities that result when people inhabit our completed designs. Successful outcomes and positive experiences demonstrate the value of architecture and public spaces.

Within our portfolio of work, we are able to measure value via improved test scores, patients who heal more quickly, increased attendances, or a more vibrant downtown catalyzed by new civic and cultural anchors.

The perspective bird's-eye view is one of our favorite tools for illustrating the first journey into a project. This drawing of the Lagoon Explora in Rio de Janeiro [see figure 6] is simultaneously a treasure hunt, conversation starter, and representation of the research and discussions that took place between stakeholder and architect. We used this drawing (and those in figures 1, 2, 3, 4, and 25) to journey into the imagination of our patrons as a response to the previously elusive questions "como é que se parece?" ("what does it look like?"), and "como vamos fazer isso?" ("how will we do that?"). In the design process, these journeys reveal opportunities and help to tell the stories about the value that design brings into everyday life. Embedding opportunities for varied outcomes for people to approach our work from multiple perspectives, and creating value for a community (however they may measure it), are what we do daily at Architecture Is Fun. This book features many iconic projects from our practice, accompanied by the stories that enrich and give each their own meaning.

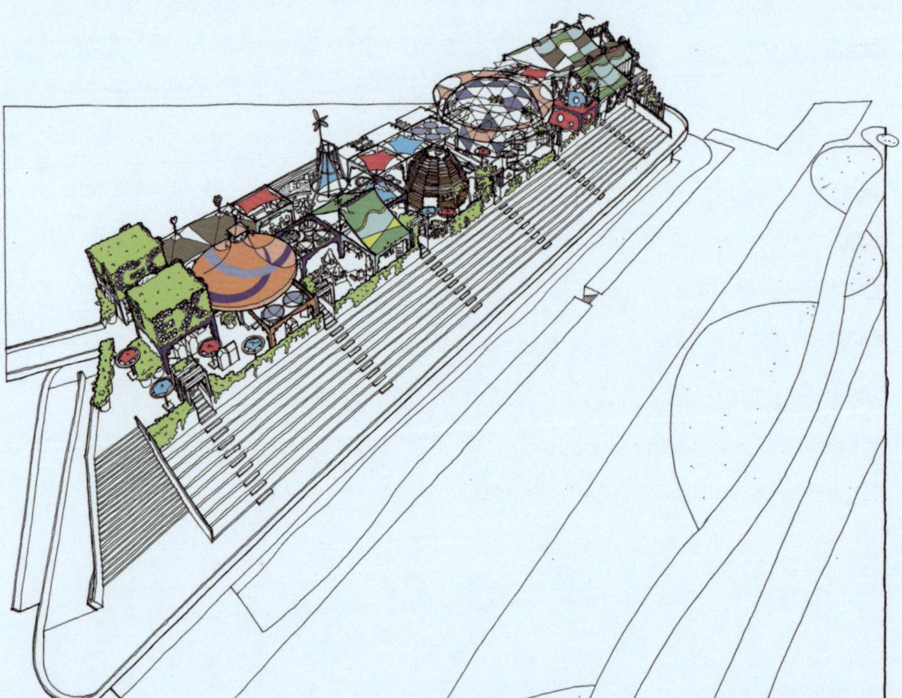

Figure 6 Lagoon Explora | Rio de Janeiro, Brazil

STORYTELLING: LINKING DRAWING AND DIRECTION

Drawing plays a major role in our storytelling process. Many of our favorite stories are the picture books of our childhoods. Richard Scarry's *Busy, Busy World*, JM Barrie's *Peter Pan*, Charles Schultz's *Peanuts*, and Raymond Briggs's *Fungus the Bogeyman* are among our favorites. Studies show that 90 percent of the population will create almost 100 percent of the drawings they will make in their lifetimes before the age of ten. Likely that age threshold coincides with many adults suggesting our attention be turned over to vocational pursuits that favor logic and linear thinking, over art and imagination.

Thankfully, we still draw. We use drawing as a process to explore and sustain the innate curiosity we all have as children. To paraphrase the landscape architect Lady Allen of Hurtwood, one of the twentieth-century's greatest champions of play, drawing is one of a series of vivid and habitual childhood gifts. *If dimmed, such talents may never reappear.* Allen crusaded to create playgrounds as sympathetic environments in which such gifts could flourish and have importance for future careers and happiness. Drawing is one of our essential tools of exploration and communication.

We love picture books because they help connect observations with reason, linking concepts with words. Illustrations are artful. Not mere decoration to text, illustrations are evocative and they enhance storytelling.

For Architecture Is Fun, sketching, diagramming, and mapping help us illustrate ideas in straightforward and accessible ways. Through the act of making drawings we can share our client stories in easily understood and appreciated ways to propel the design process.

For Young At Art Museum, drawing and storytelling became an organizing methodology of using art for learning. We used the analogy of transit maps to simplify a complex set of requirements and to identify what art-making happens where.

Figure 7 Young At Art Museum | Davie, Florida

Figure 8 Young At Art Museum | Davie, Florida

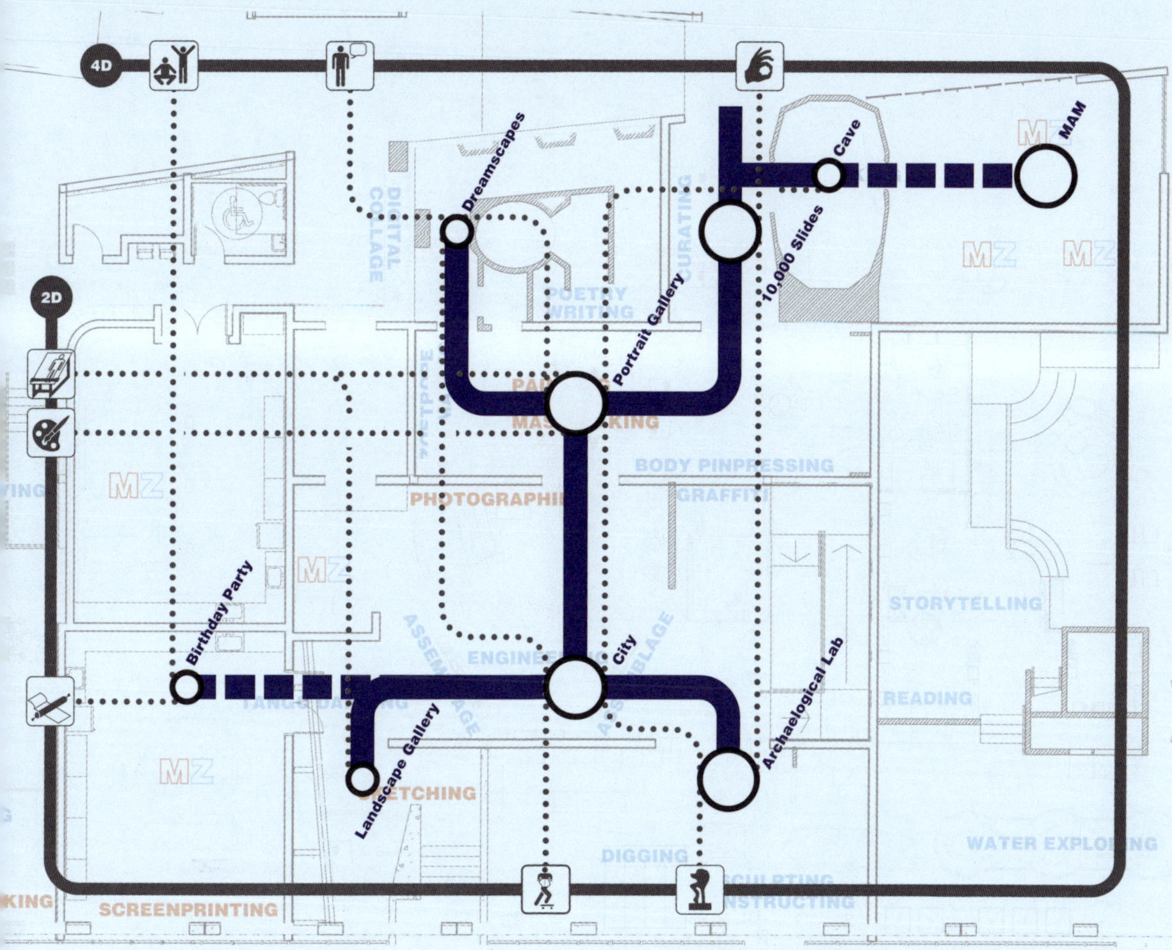

Figure 9 Young At Art Museum | Davie, Florida

Mapping each of the four core galleries, we created district lines, showing "stops" along the way that correspond to art-making experiences [see figures 7, 8]. When combined, art-making, process, and product are mapped across the museum to ensure an equitable distribution of activity across galleries, aligned with curatorial stories and goals. The final map in the series [see figure 9] overlays the transit system onto a more conventional architectural plan, color-coding experiences, the journeys of making, and visitor wayfinding.

Figure 10 Art Institute of Chicago | Chicago, Illinois

For the Art Institute of Chicago, a similar map made the fractured logistics of arrival and needs of diverse user groups legible [see figures 11, 12, 13]. This analytical approach allows us to make complex network systems intelligible and to predict better ways of mapping how people may behave in spaces. When we add research of visitor flow, both intended and unintended, we can demonstrate a more intuitive and inviting museum journey to our client. Using design in this way often results in the experience of coming to an art museum for the first time less confusing and less intimidating. Equity and access within the built environment are essential architectural outcomes of our methodology of storytelling.

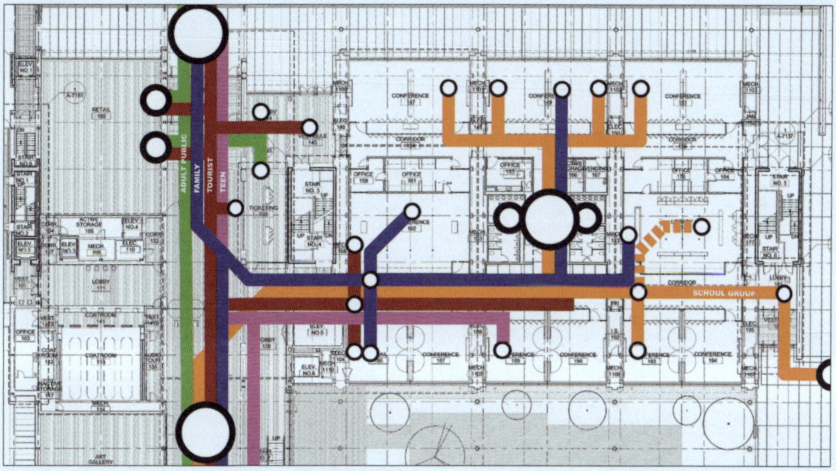

Figure 11 Art Institute of Chicago | Chicago, Illinois

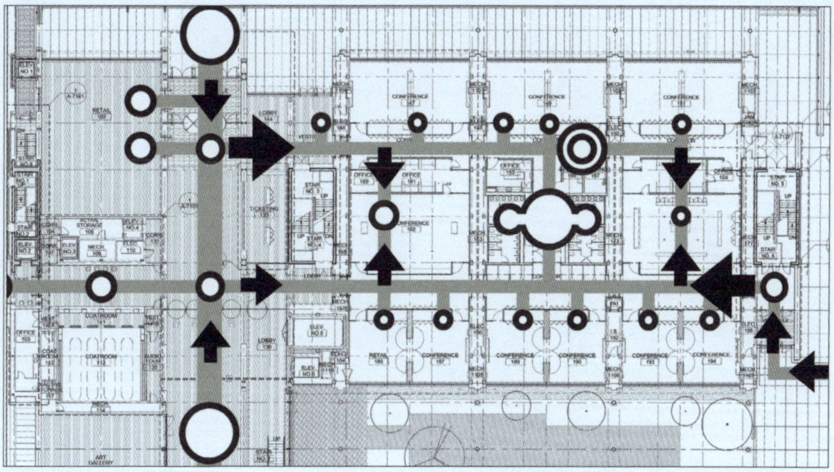

Figure 12 Art Institute of Chicago | Chicago, Illinois

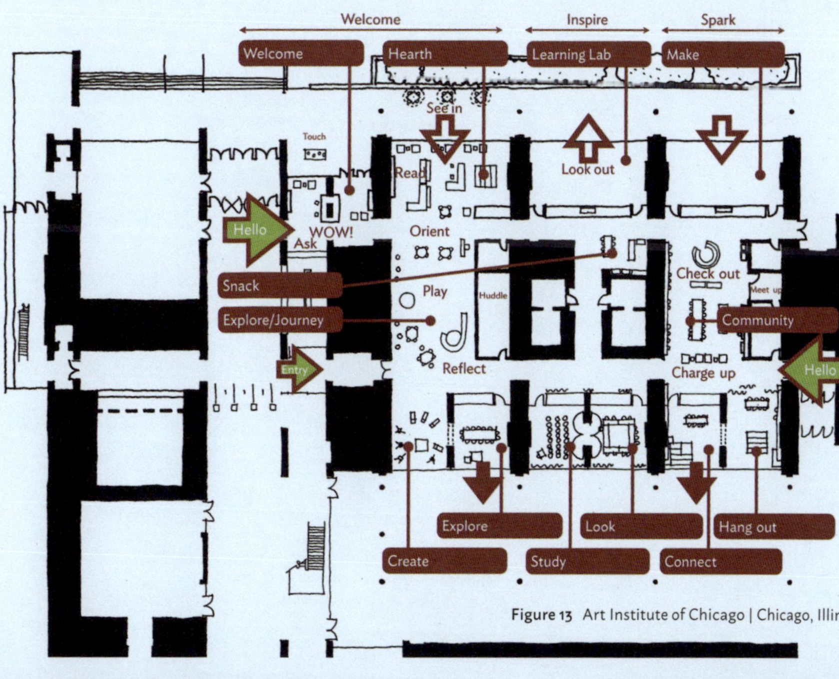

Figure 13 Art Institute of Chicago | Chicago, Illinois

A PUBLIC SPACE TOOLKIT

These two-dimensional system diagrams are useful for seeing potential solutions to wayfinding, flow, and navigation, or to illustrate opportunities for flexibility, access, and optimum use within the network. When we introduce spatial qualities to these drawings, they become powerful storytelling tools to fuel imaginations and confirm our findings. We believe that the best public spaces come about when strong architectural ideas are conceived alongside ideas of experience, flexibility, artfulness, and surprise.

We've compared great public spaces with a favorite breakfast cereal. Simple cardboard boxes (representing the basic architectural idea) are enriched and emblazoned with characters on the front, while puzzles and activities are printed on the back [see figure 14]. Inside the box is the delicious sugar-coated cereal, and sometimes a hermetically sealed plastic novelty waiting to be discovered.

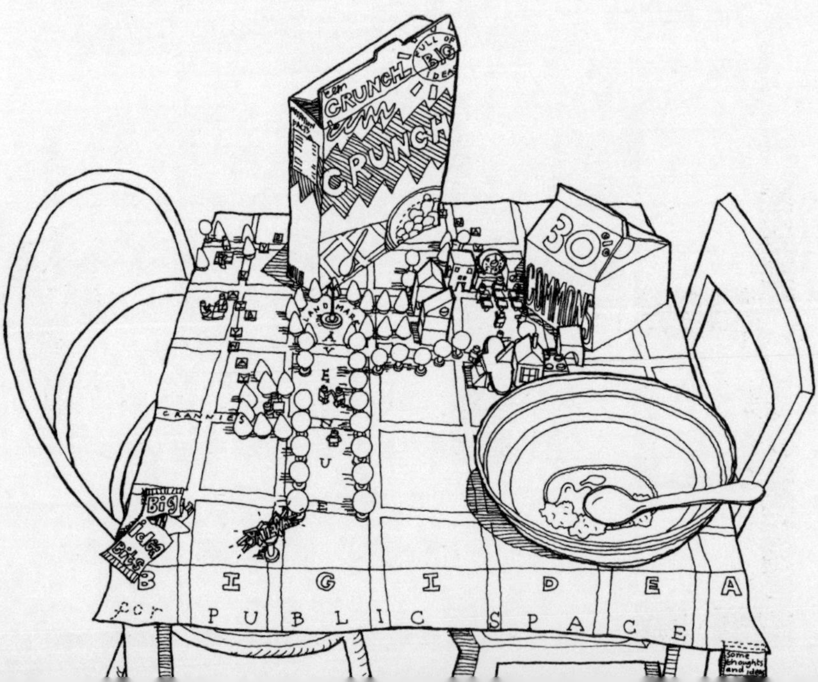

Figure 14 Cereal Box

We have applied this metaphor to buildings, interiors, and other public spaces with a series of tactics diagrammed within our *Building Experience Spectrum* [see figures 15, 16, 17]:

- Simple enclosures are made more interesting with openings and connections to views or pathways.
- Furnishings and arrangements of other objects allow opportunities for community engagement.
- Materials and visual adornment create a sense of beauty and well-being.
- Introducing and layering a thoughtful complexity readies a basic space for activity and engagement. Some of this may be through interactivity and playful interventions.
- Anticipating variation and flexibility invites people to use the space in different and rewarding ways. Such flexibility is enriched by time and seasonality.
- Art very often enhances the experience.

Being conscious of these tactics in the design process provides a framework to develop the intersection of space, experience, and art for any building or environment. Using this *Building Experience Spectrum* is a very useful tool for us as we imagine the pathways, nooks, crannies, commons, benches, and play places that are the hallmarks of a memorable public space. Our drawings are often annotated with this language to make them more accessible, and to prompt stories and scenarios of the experiences that will happen in the places we design. This toolkit can also be applied in post-occupancy evaluations to determine degrees of success, and to inform future adjustments.

SPATIAL DEFINITION

EMBRACING AND SHELTERING

Public spaces can be formal and organized, embraced by planes, objects, volumes, surfaces, openings, and details. These compositions generate shelter, comfort, and a sense of place connected to physical and social contexts.

PROGRAMMATIC MATING

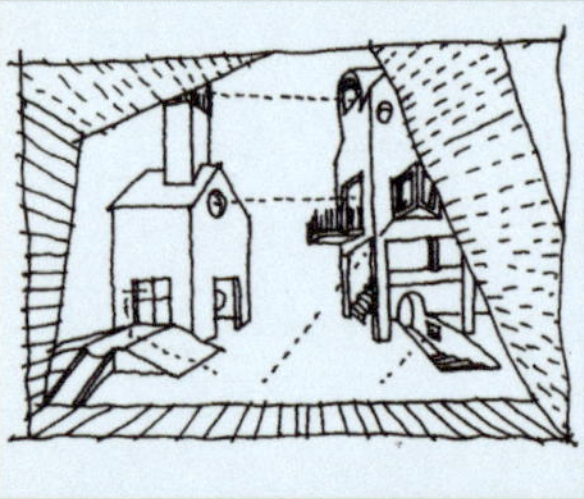

LINKING AND CONNECTING

The simple or complex ways in which architectural elements are juxtaposed can generate access, links, circulation arrangements, and enhance visual connections, making public spaces more interesting and animated.

LIVING STREET

SHARING AND ENCOURAGING

By introducing communal seating and other shared elements, public spaces can be made more informal, which encourages a sense of community and interaction.

EMOTIVE BEAUTY

FEELING AND SENSING

Public spaces can be emotive: they can feel beautiful, and they can challenge the senses with artistic, visual, or any other stimuli.

URBAN GAMES

PLAYING AND INVITING

Hosting invitational events within public spaces can create active engagement and memorable play shared between family, friends, and strangers.

PURPOSEFUL UTILIZATION

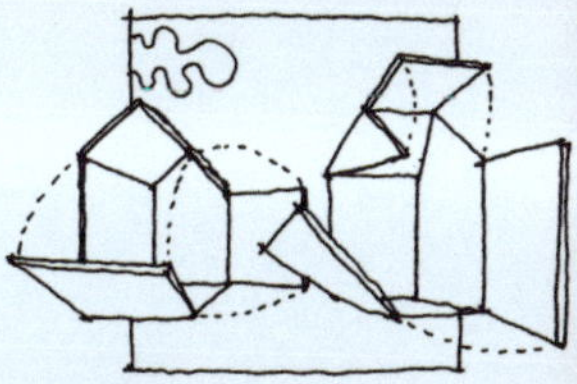

ADAPTING AND VARYING

Public spaces can be more effective when they adapt and host different events and experiences concurrently or at varying times.

DYNAMIC SEASONALITY

CHANGING AND SURPRISING

Changes in the weather, schedule, or seasons alongside ever-changing phenomenon, from happenings to celebrations can create invigorated public spaces.

MIND BODY PROVOCATION

ASKING AND WONDERING

Encountering the unexpected within public spaces stimulates inquiry and kindles wonder, fuels the imagination, and challenges mind and body experiences.

Figure 15 Building Experience Spectrum

LIVING STREET

Plaza populated with benches, facing an interactive art wall

DYNAMIC SEASONALITY

A topiary maze installation activates the museum's rooftop greenspace

WAYFINDING AND GRAPHICS

Artist-in-residence creates an ever-changing entry supergraphic

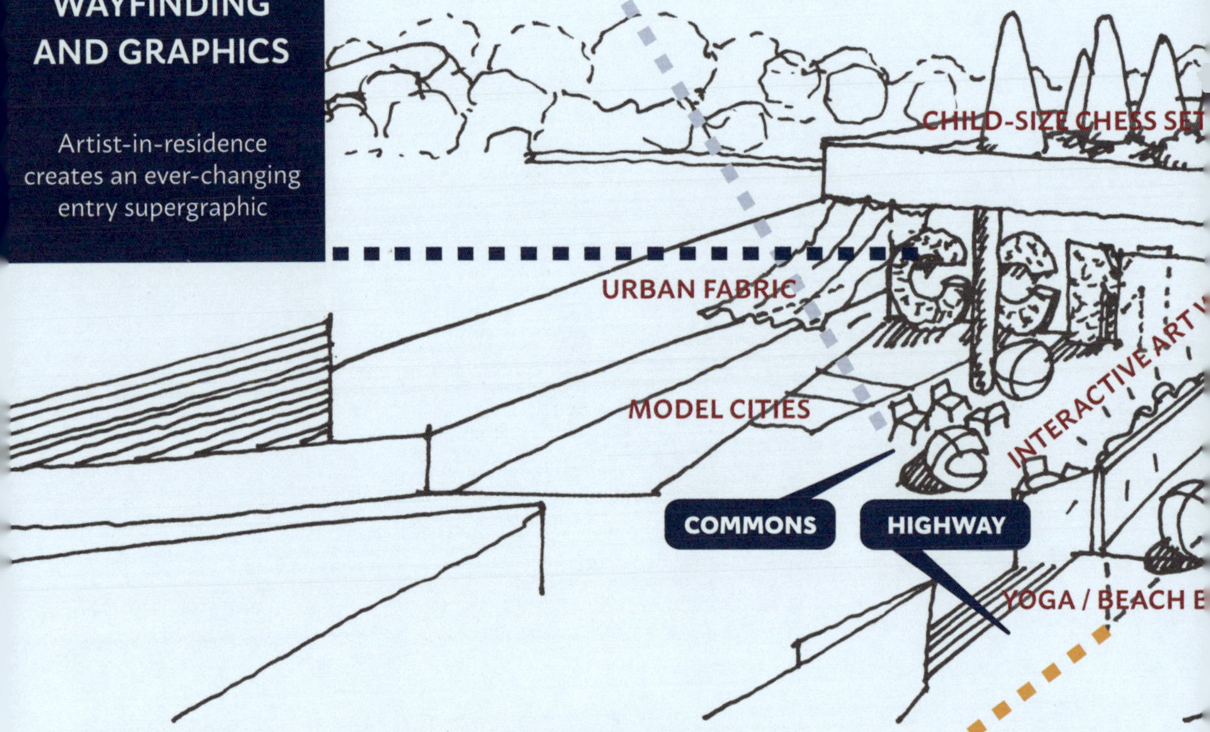

MIND BODY PROVOCATION

Mysterious portals and openings into the museum below spark inquiry and wonder

PROGRAMMATIC MATING

Views into the museum activity below connect the activated exterior with the interior, making learning and play visible

Figure 16 Applying public space tactics at Chicago Children's Museum

EMOTIVE BEAUTY

Urban fabric, draping arrival sequence along Randolph Street sidewalk

PURPOSEFUL UTILIZATION

Public platform staging arrival events, including guitar-playing troubadours

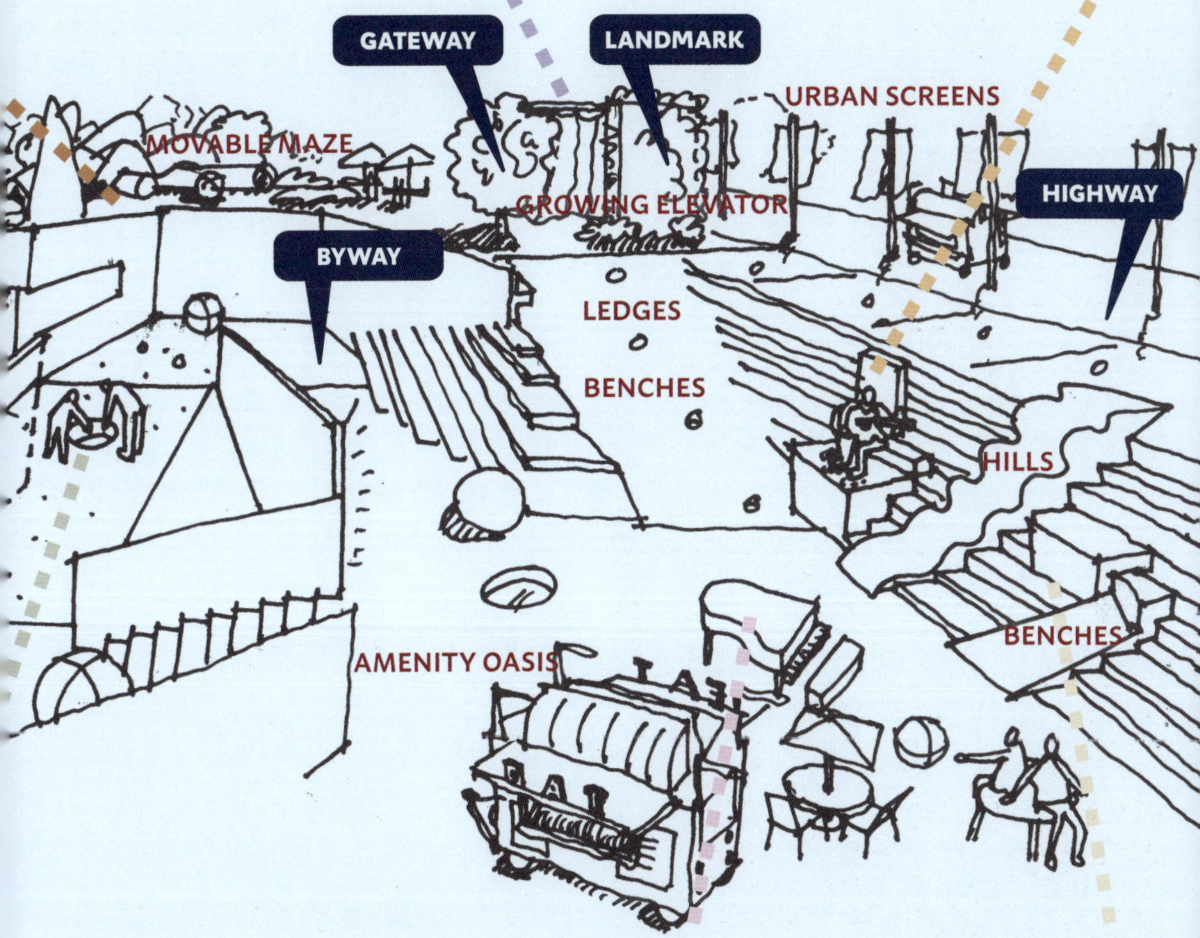

URBAN GAMES

A public piano invites impromptu performance and spontaneous musical events

SPATIAL DEFINITION

Formal yet playful stair interventions embrace and encourage family socialization

GRAND APPROACH

— Seeing and Sensing —

The Grand Approach is the child's gateway and access to play and learning—it imparts a sense of order and proportion (to perhaps a chaotic urban fabric). The gateway is an eloquent expression of the museum's place within the culture of the city. The Grand Approach creates vistas that are the museum's stories of the flow of space, structure, celebration, and energy found within. The Grand Approach is mesmerizing; its grand impression elevates a child's sense of self. Its avenues transport you—shifting perspective from where you were to where you are going. Its landmarks signify its place within the city and your heart. The Grand Approach moves you and motivates you—it is about seeing that this is for you and sensing why you are here.

Nutrition Facts

Serving Size: 1 Museum Visit
Servings Per Container: Unlimited

Tactical Alignments	
Spatial definition	30%
Programmatic mating	
Living street	50%
Emotive beauty	0%
Urban games	0%
Purposeful utilization	0%
Dynamic seasonality	5%
Mind body provocation	0%
Tactical Enrichments	
Spatial definition	0%
Programmatic mating	10%
Living street	0%
Emotive beauty	20%
Urban games	40%
Purposeful utilization	5%
Dynamic seasonality	5%
Mind body provocation	20%
Big Idea Enablers	
Gateways	40%
Avenues	30%
Landmarks	25%
Commons	0%
Crannies	0%
Byways	5%
Pit stops	0%
Big Idea Tenets	
Welcoming	40%
Guiding	5%
Feeling comfortable	20%
Linking to museum experiences	5%
Inspiring meaningful play	5%
Inspiring memories	15%
Inspiring understanding	10%

Figure 17 An exemplar of public space tactics applied to children's museums

GATEWAYS
Openings, Entry, Front Door, Stairs
Greeting, Showing up, Meeting, Sitting, Viewing, Sensing

GATEWAYS
Porte-cochère, Foyer, Lobby
Extending welcome, Energizing, Mingling, Meeting, Be in the party

LANDMARKS
Identifiers, Stairs, Banners, Vendor Carts
Marking the grounds, Eating, Snacking, Filling up, Participating

LANDMARKS
Decorative Devices & Ornament
Being looked after, Celebrating, Distinguishing

LANDMARKS
Signifiers, Identifying Locations
Hosting, Promoting, Advertising

LANDMARKS
Symbols & Guides: Scale and Porte-cochère
Welcoming, Surprising, Arriving, Guiding

AVENUES
Yards
Open to new adventures, Joining in, Taking part

LANDMARKS
Scale
Making monumental moments, Participating

EMBEDDING RESEARCH IN DESIGN

For up to 20,000 visitors every day, the experience of arriving at the Field Museum in Chicago likely began as part of a crowd facing a bewildering number of ticketing options. This distracted from the impressive architectural arrival in one of America's most majestic interior spaces: the act of looking up and the excitement at the prospect of being in one of the world's greatest natural history museums were relegated. In helping the Field Museum with this public space challenge, our research-driven recommendations were subtractive, suggesting that good design in the public interest might be fewer design interventions done more thoughtfully.

To create openness and accessibility, we relied on understanding and modulating pedestrian patterns and healthy public space attributes. One of our first tasks was to map every sign and instruction greeting visitors in Stanley Field Hall (inspired by some of the drawings in Venturi, Scott Brown and Izenour's 1972 book *Learning From Las Vegas*). Such a drawing was daunting, as was the experience for museum visitors; there were literally hundreds of written pieces of information—small, large, formal, and ad-hoc signs, banners, electronic maps, et al [see figure 18]. Communicating this complexity relies upon the storyboarding approach, the annotation of real-time photographs, and three-dimensional illustrations of the Great Hall shown in these examples [see figures 19, 20, 21].

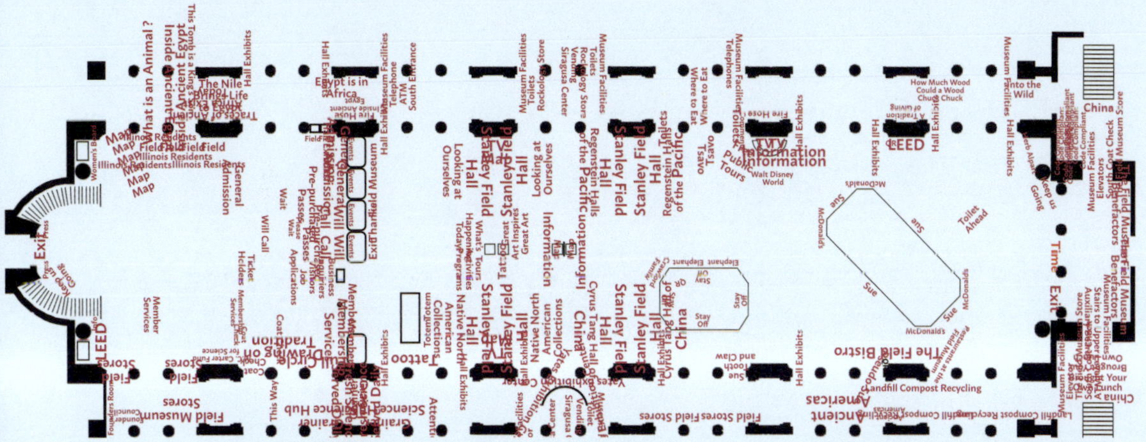

Figure 18 Stanley Field Hall, Field Museum | Chicago, Illinois

igure 19 Stanley Field Hall, ield Museum | Chicago, Iwllinois

At the Field Museum, we consider the optimization of data as an integral component of the architect's arsenal of tools. Evidence-based design is one the key components of the relationship we have with the museum. They are scientists, first and foremost, and it is a reasonable expectation on their part that Architecture Is Fun's work is validated through research and quantifiable outcomes. Using methods like the toolbox creates a more persuasive case for the value of design and its impact on the bottom line of resilience, sustainability, economics, and visitor engagement. This process and illustrated documentation showed how the public space could enable happier staff and visitors, a more mission critical experience and a more efficient museum. Happiness is measured through post-interviews; one example from an educator on the museum floor noted that new configurations allowed for far more meaningful interactions with visitors, whereas previously their role had been to direct visitors to bathrooms or other amenities.

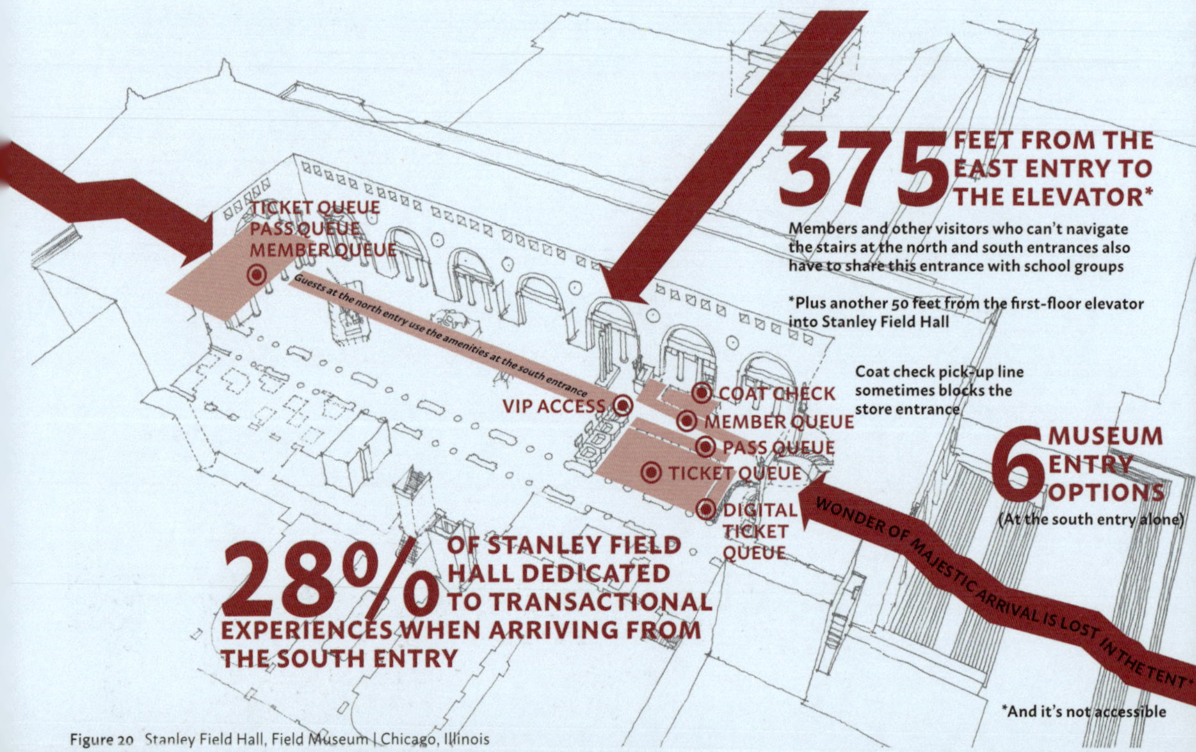

Figure 20 Stanley Field Hall, Field Museum | Chicago, Illinois

We devised a series of experimental prototype layouts, which were tested in controlled conditions. These proved that a subtractive design approach better oriented visitors, made for an easier and calmer entry, and opened up this grand public space. This successful data-based approach enabled the museum to concentrate more on communicating its mission, and less time correcting logistical snafus caused by earlier, less deliberate design decisions.

For the record, virtually every sign and notice has been removed from Stanley Field Hall. The lack of clutter is conspicuous and navigation is much clearer. Originally 28 percent of the floor area of Stanley Field Hall was taken up in the experience of transactional exchanges (queuing and buying tickets, or checking coats). Our solution reduces that figure to less than 10 percent [see figures 22, 23, 24], and provides a free and open experience for all. Less is more.

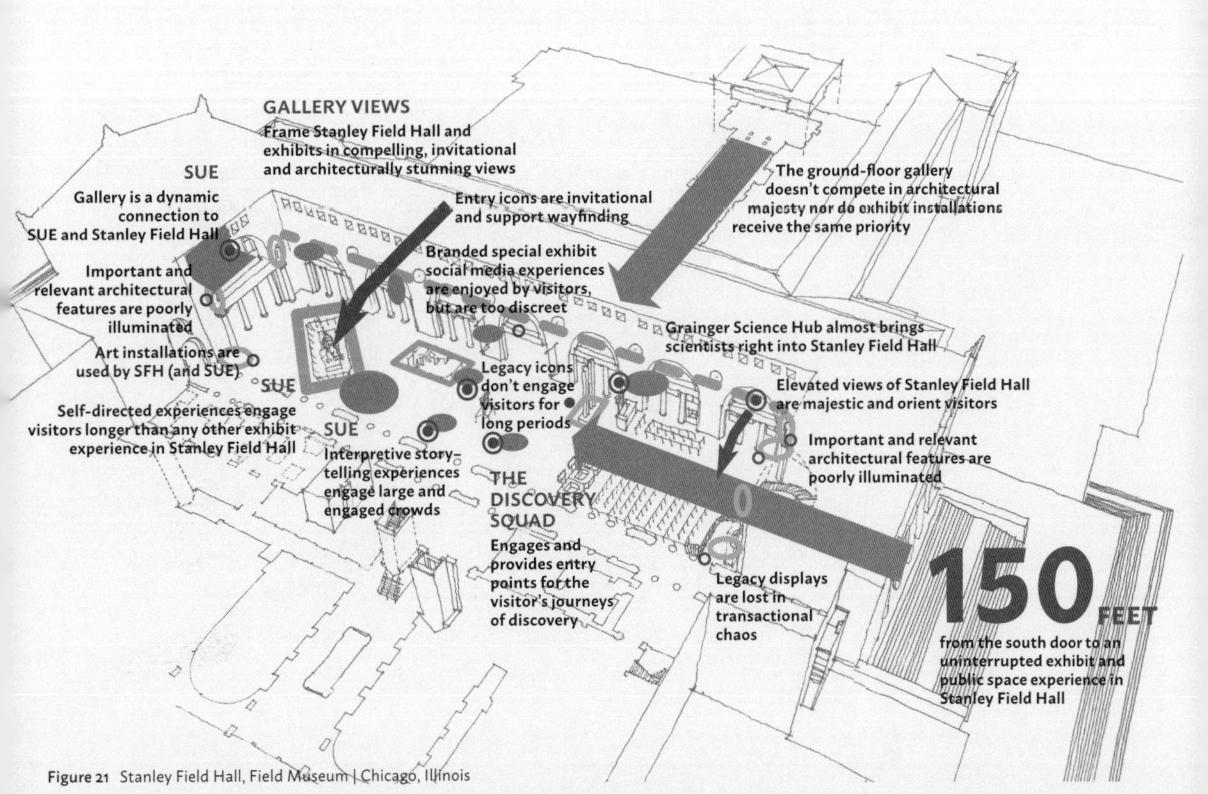

Figure 21 Stanley Field Hall, Field Museum | Chicago, Illinois

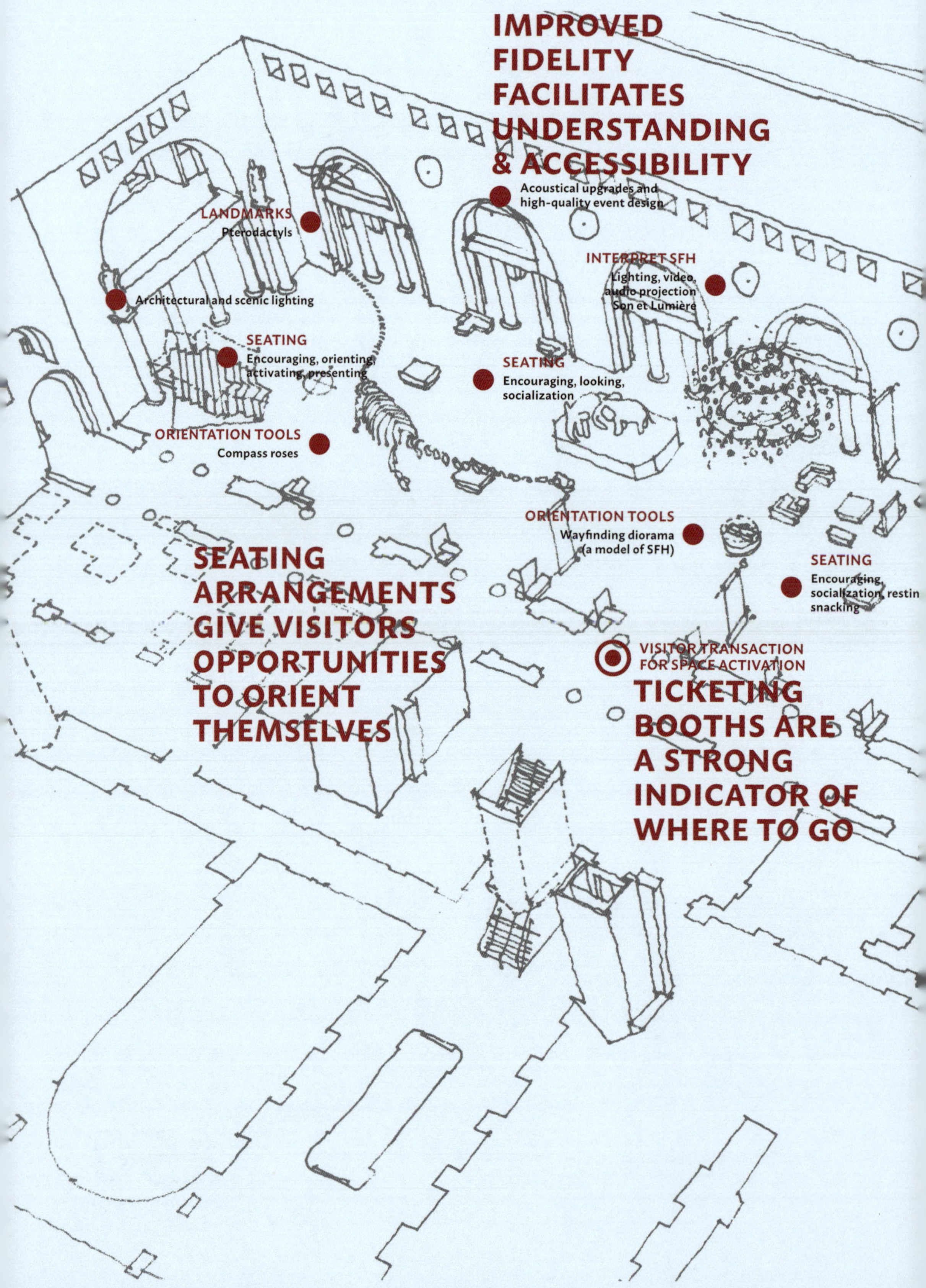

Figure 22 Stanley Field Hall, Field Museum | Chicago, Illinois

COMPREHENSIVE, CONSISTENT, CONSPICUOUS, CLEAR, AND EYE-CATCHING MESSAGES SUPPORT WAYFINDING

ACCENTED FEATURES ACT AS LANDMARKS AND VISUAL CUES

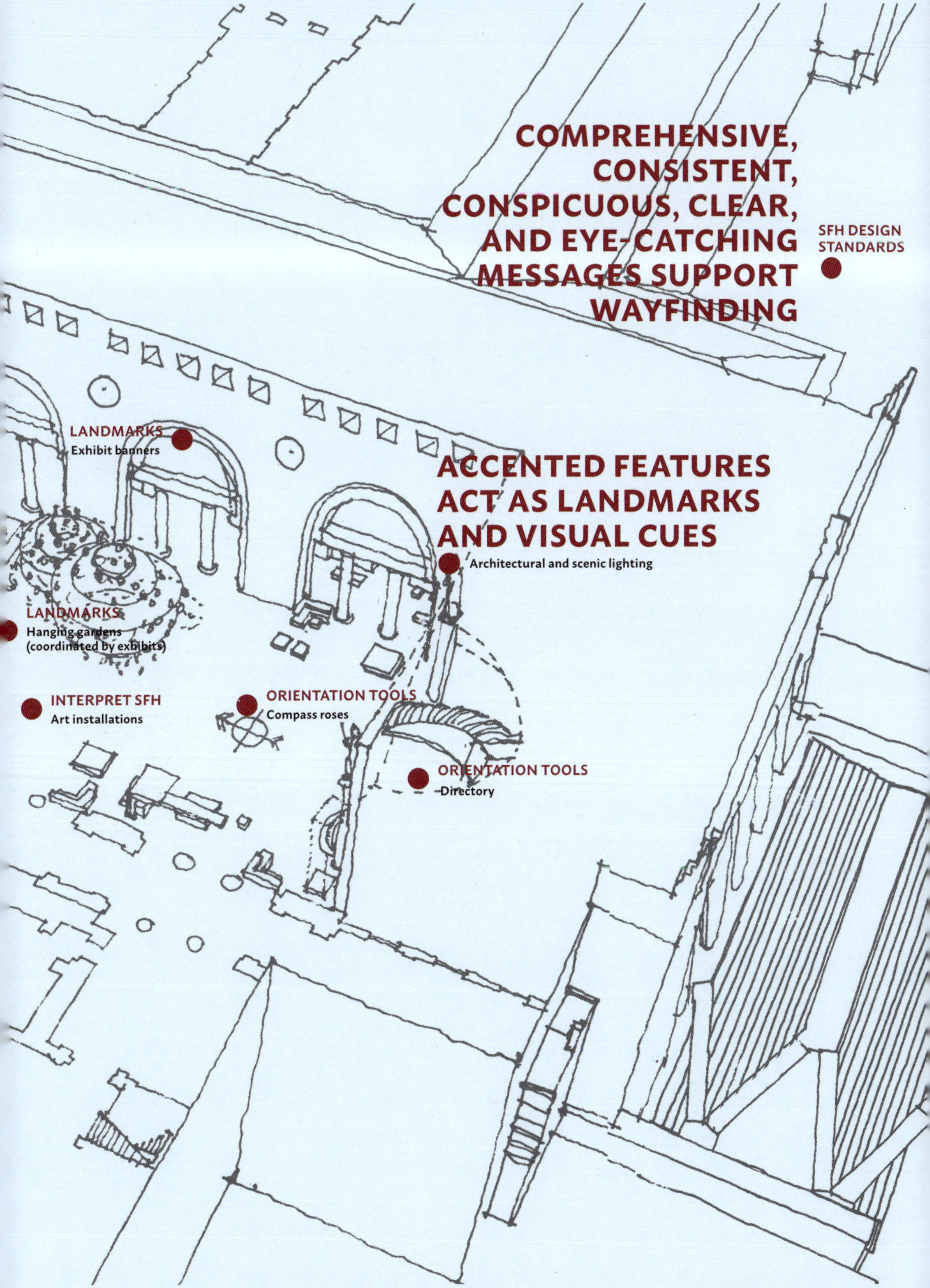

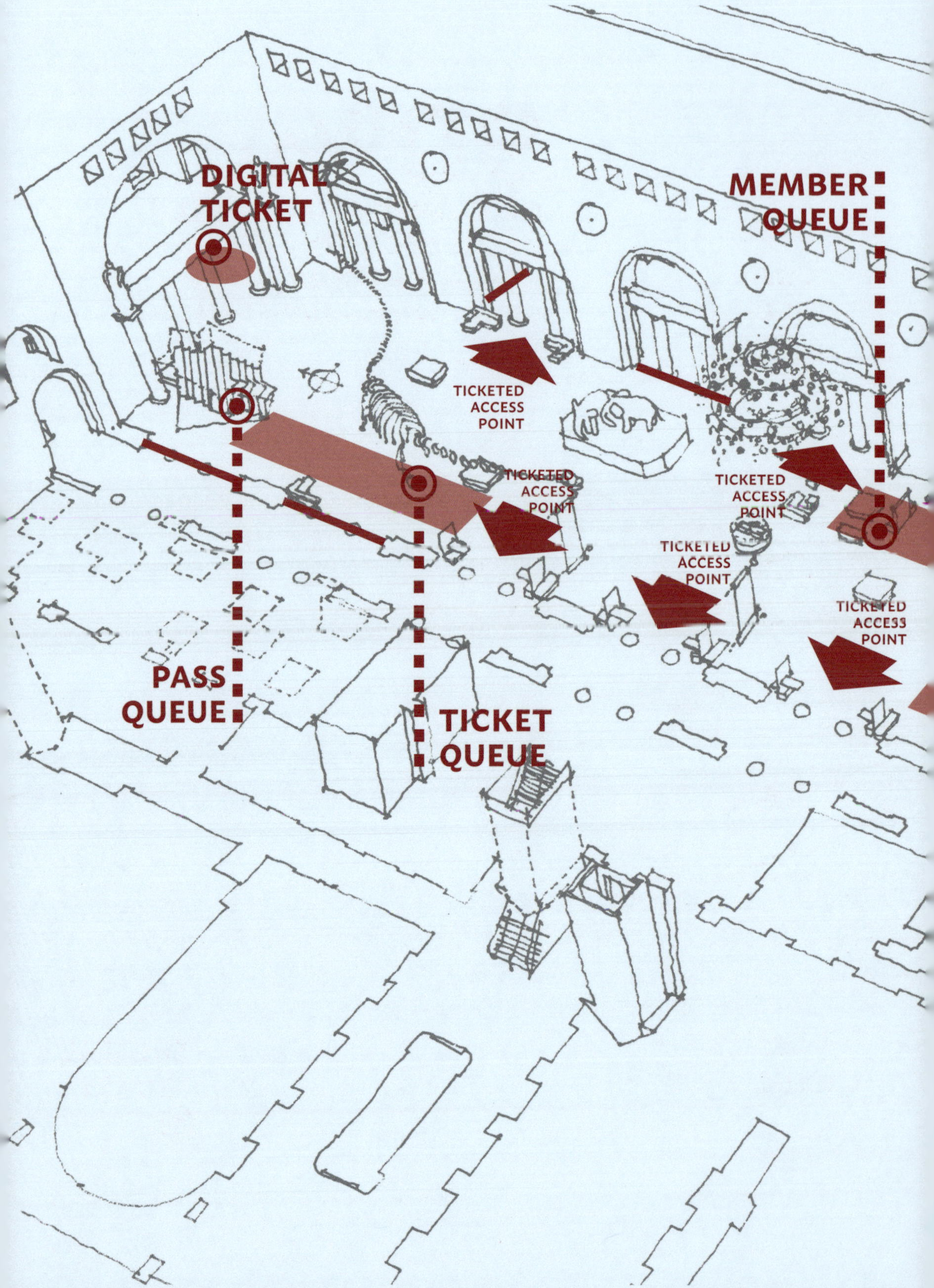

Figure 23 Stanley Field Hall, Field Museum | Chicago, Illinois

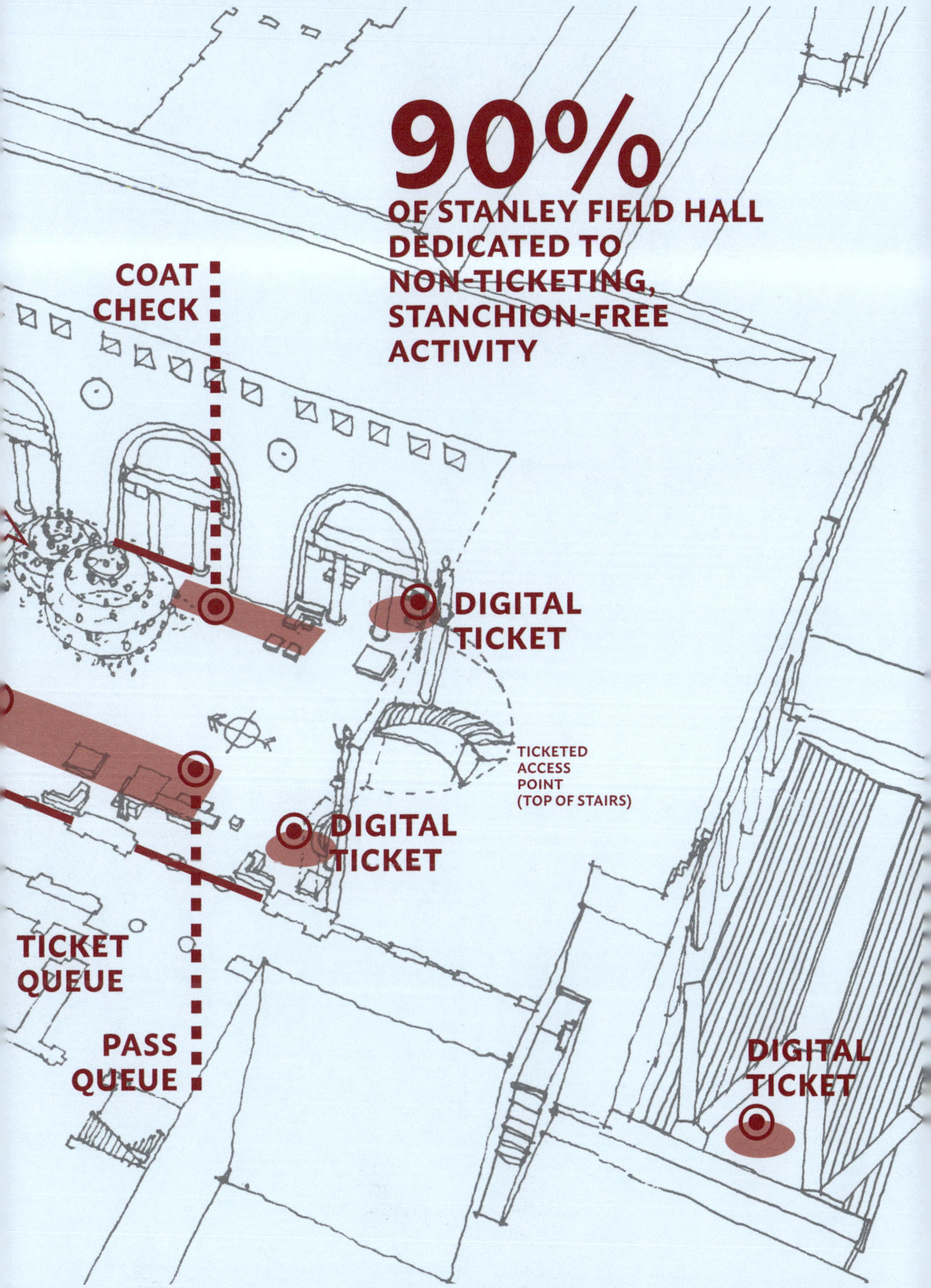
90%
OF STANLEY FIELD HALL DEDICATED TO NON-TICKETING, STANCHION-FREE ACTIVITY
COAT CHECK
DIGITAL TICKET
TICKETED ACCESS POINT (TOP OF STAIRS)
DIGITAL TICKET
TICKET QUEUE
PASS QUEUE
DIGITAL TICKET

Figure 24 Stanley Field Hall, Field Museum | Chicago, Illinois

MAKING EVERYDAY LIFE MORE FUN

Here follows a series of projects by our firm, Architecture Is Fun, where design and storytelling play a major role. There is a richness to the exhibits, museums, schools, libraries, themed environments, and other places in this book emanating from the missions or goals of each of the organizations, institutions, and clients who invited us to design their spaces. The examples expressed in this essay are concentrated in the early conceptual and schematic stages of design, envisioning, and planning. Every project of ours begins with a series of drawings, which illustrate places where these principles, strategies, and tools are leveraged to give ideas their physical form.

We use research to figure out functional conundrums, to inform solutions to architectural and pragmatic challenges, and to solve inherent constraints prioritized in a defined program. These initial designs are the moment where we (architects alongside our stakeholder collaborators) craft, edit, and develop the story that brands an environment.

We enjoy the development and documentation of a project where ideation shifts gears and is in harmony with all the pragmatic criteria and a reality of execution; this is a phase where we continue as the staunchest of advocates for story, where imagination turns into a reality.

In the heart of this book are the illustrations and stories representing completed projects. We have grouped these finished works by typology or thematic ideas, versus a chronology, and we hope this arrangement of our adventures in design validates your curiosity and justifies your interest and investigation.

From PlayMaze on, all of our projects apply the strategies and tactics described in this essay to help attract and engage people to play, learn, explore, and experience these places in ways that are relevant to them, and in ways that even we did not imagine.

This is our story.

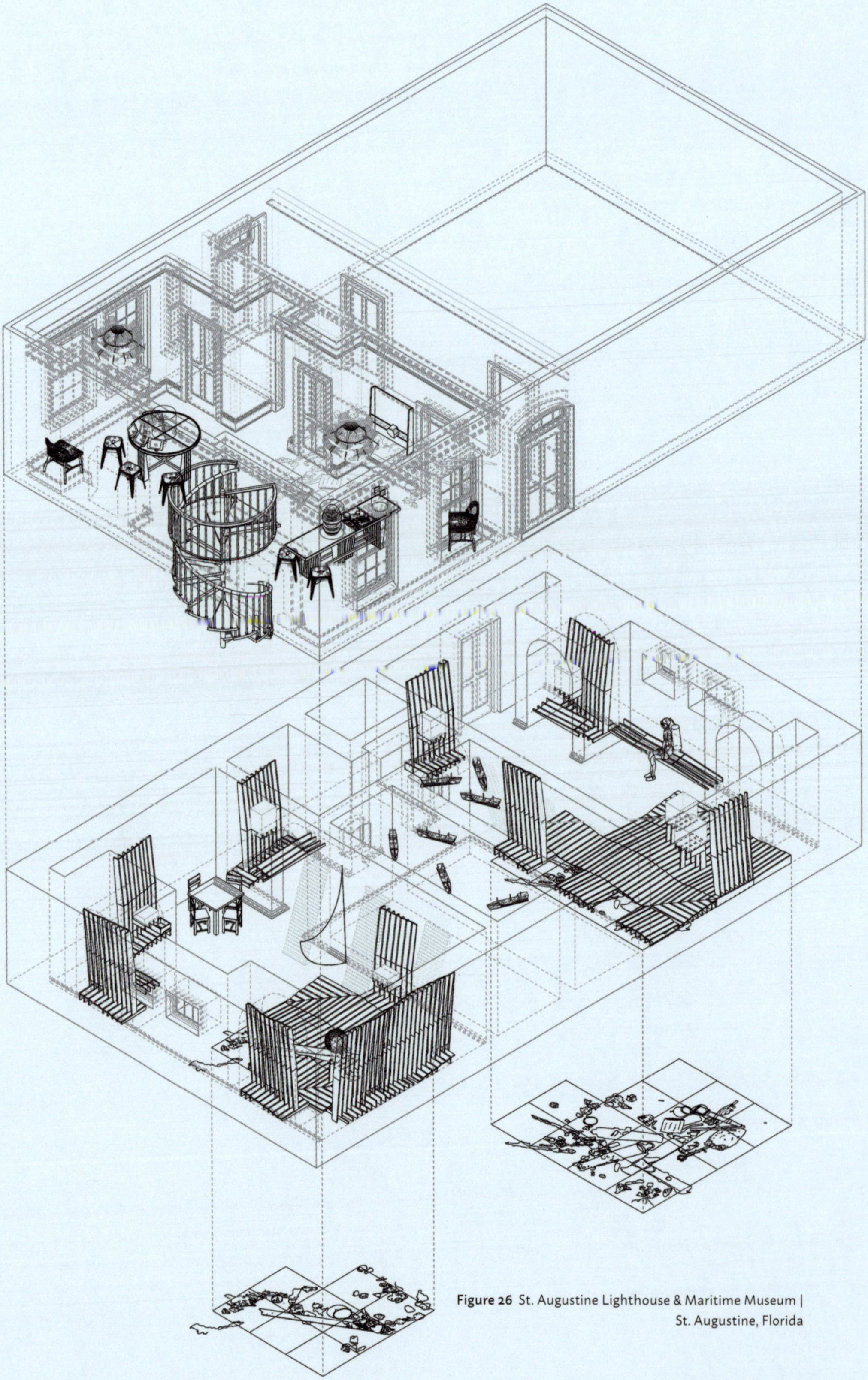

Figure 26 St. Augustine Lighthouse & Maritime Museum | St. Augustine, Florida

CASE STUDIES

HEALING HEARTS AND MINDS AWAY FROM HOME

Building a warm, nurturing home in the woods for families of seriously ill children, we demonstrate the critical message of how architecture creates significant value of support, socialization, and shared experience. Our House in the Woods, a Ronald McDonald House, provides anxious families a place of refuge and respite. The three-story green-and-gold cottage is nestled carefully among a grove of trees, expressing the very essence of home. A circular drive features a slender porte-cochère, whose canopy wraps around an embracing tree and shelters visitors directly to the front door. The porte-cochère's green roof reduces heating and cooling costs and lessens stormwater run-off in a flood area.

It was critical that our design reach out; patient rooms across the street look directly to the house. Children can see their families. We took great care with the imagery and the plan, which is literally depicted like open arms. Iconographic and symbolic elements help the 21,000-square-foot, sixteen-bedroom house feel like home.

Families intuitively navigate a layout that features an expanded kitchen, dining room, living room, and grand staircase, which winds around a three-story fireplace. This healthy home offers intimate nooks and crannies where families under stress can feel reprieve. The chef-style kitchen with rounded buffet accommodates the continual flow of volunteers, while bookend cooking zones allow individualized family use. A reuse of Forest Stewardship Council–certified antique wood flooring warms the public spaces; Energy Star appliances, natural content furnishings and fabrics, and low-flow fixtures are responsible and economical. Each year, the healing House in the Woods hosts over 750 families supported by over 45,000 volunteer hours.

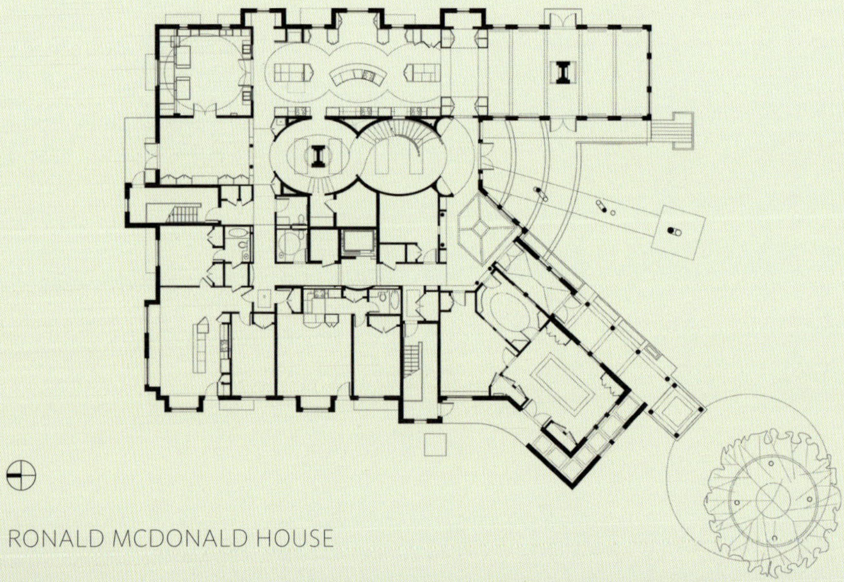

WALKING IN THE WOODS CONNECTS NATURE AND HOME

Our design is a modern mash-up of learning environments and landscapes, and a synthesis of indoors and out-of-doors. The resulting destination is fun to explore and a great place to return to. The unique integration of a man-made interior forest, landscape, animal habitats, and multi-generational experiences create an extraordinary, safe, and accessible walk in the woodlands for visitors of all ages and learning styles.

Among structural tree trunks, our canopy climber of curved poplar plywood, a collaboration with artist Tom Luckey, allows zoo-goers to soar 22 feet into the air. Webs of silver cable safely nestle children as they ascend to discover the best views of the patterned terrariums and aviary below. Elsewhere, our extra-large viewing windows and touch-tanks permit closer looks at animals while related activities, like the beaver water table, connect a hands-on experience with habitats. In a city where winter is long, the interior conveys an eternal springtime, enhanced by natural illumination and an impressive outside view.

The clearing and interpretive pylons along the woodland walk are crafted educational devices. Made of steel branches, the bronzed clearing canopy opens up into an arena perfect for programs, performances, or rest. The pylons inform visitors about the animals and their habitats in multiple ways, each with a corresponding hands-on interactive to observe and experience.

Through art, architecture, and habitat, visitors come to appreciate our natural world and gain a better understanding of the animals sharing our locale and our ecosystem.

IMPROVING TEST SCORES THROUGH PUBLIC SPACE DESIGN

High-school faculty, alumni, and students challenged us to transform a ubiquitous pass-through space into a hub for interaction and innovation. The result is a public space integrating science as a social act and amplifying the curriculum experientially and exponentially. An Eames and Kees Boeke–inspired *Powers of Ten* mural introduces curricula-appropriate concepts of scale, space, and perspective, promoting learning through touch and experience. Similarly, the morphing bench artfully demonstrates a DNA strand; flexible riser seating doubles as curiosity cabinets of teaching specimens; the ceiling houses a model of fusion; while the flooring demonstrates the *Golden Mean*, with its one-meter grid for measurement and calibration used in experiments of testing laws of motion and inertia.

Experientially, our design is a technology-rich center, an extra classroom, a speaker space, an enhanced exploratory zone, and a recruitment asset. Exponentially, the cost-effective forum is a place for investigation and inquiry for students and faculty alike. In its first year, this public space was a pivotal factor in 29 percent more girls enrolling in Advanced Placement Science and test scores increasing by 37 percent, contributing to a higher percentage of college enrollments and first-choice acceptances.

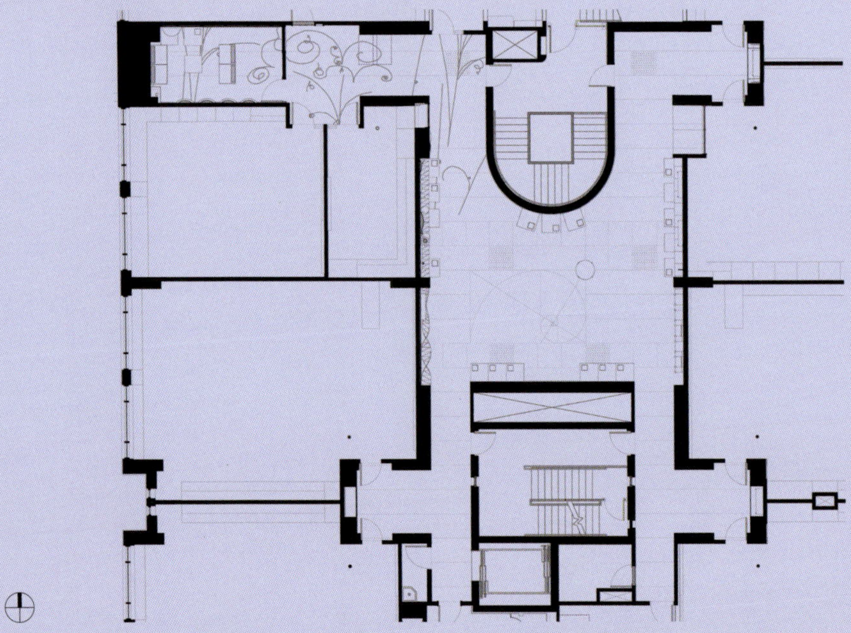

"Truth emerges more readily from error than from confusion"
—Bacon

DESIGNING A SOCIALLY INVENTIVE EPICENTER OF ART AND DISCOVERY

Simultaneously artful and art-filled, Young At Art Museum defines a new sector of museums. Taking a sophisticated and outward-facing design approach, our design bridges the gap between an adult art museum and the underappreciated children's museum typology. This openness is reflected within 22,000 square feet of transformative public space and galleries that express welcome and play.

During the envisioning process, we convened a symposium and roundtables where experts from Museum of Modern Art (in New York), The Getty Museum, Noguchi Museum, Chicago Children's Museum, Brooklyn Museum of Art, and Museum for African Art helped inform content and context. Parents, educators, artists, cultural groups, children, and teens from across South Florida contributed their insights during ideation. Our approach was imaginative, yet pragmatic. With an unwavering commitment to over six years of design with this client, we listened and were open to dialogue. While art museums and children's museums share the same values and approaches to nurturing the next generation of those who will embrace the arts and keep art vital, we believed it was imperative to define a new sector of twenty-first century museums—the art museum for children. Upon opening its doors, Young At Art raised its national profile for excellence and leadership, and achieved the highest national recognition with accreditation from the American Association of Museums.

We created four core galleries, and collaborations with over thirty-five renowned artists that connect art with experience, seeing with critical thinking, and art objects with art-making: *ArtScapes* repositions art and its histories; *NatureScapes* calls attention to caring for our environment; *CultureScapes* explores heritage and tradition; and *WonderScapes* delights in early learning.

Positioning the museum as an active participant in social opportunity, our design amplifies innovation, installation, and involvement for visitors of all ages. Imbuing 22,000 square feet of public spaces and exhibits with emotional qualities, an artful aesthetic touches the hearts of more than 150,000 visitors per year. Young At Art Museum is known as one of Florida's most innovative and inclusive arts initiatives, a facility where education and experience are considered equally through design.

GETTING ACQUAINTED WITH ART

We wanted the first impression of this art museum for children to be impactful! A contemporary cave, filled with art, music, and sensory experiences, begins the museum journey, connecting visitors to art and its histories. The Young At Art Museum's Cave, clad with super-white matte surfacing, expresses mystery and discovery, enclosure and aperture, ancient and new. It is socially engaging and cool. Interrupting a polite museum orientation gallery, the Cave draws the curious inside its intimate 250-square-foot interior.

Within, visitors make their mark, imitating early cave painting, inscribing foil panels, or using body-sized pin-presses. The artist-commissioned video supercharges the Cave as an immersive 4D flipbook of imagery, with dynamic shifts of color and an explosive score that visually captures young artists in the continuum of art history. Designed to be open for accessibility and security, the Cave's vibrant LEDs create an amazing light show.

Our design transforms the ubiquitous museum orientation gallery into an exciting experience, creating engaging public space and helping prepare children for their museum visit. Crisp and chiseled, concert-like and communicative, the Cave serves as metaphor, meeting place, orientation theater, and art-making space for visitors of all ages.

PAST
PRESENT
FUTURE

BRIDGING ENVIRONMENTAL EDUCATION THROUGH ART

A magical world of environmental education and recovered beauty at the Young At Art Museum, our *Recycling Workshop* sets the stage for creativity and acting responsibly. Museum-goers enter through large theatrical doors where Mother Earth beckons. Inspired by the poetic puppetry of Cuban-born artist Pablo Cano, the Grotto is an intimate place of orientation where the artist's touch is visible and inspiring; from the display of recycled puppets whose names flow onto the walls, to the artist's signature and thoughts incised in vinyl flooring. An upholstered video monitor presents short films in which puppets tell classic tales and rare behind-the-scene footage demonstrates the artist's transformative design process.

Environmental education programming is housed in spaces that are beautiful, imaginative, flexible, and innovative. The ordinary and the uncommon are juxtaposed in a pageantry of recycling: bins for sorting are side-by-side with old barbershop chairs made new again. The workshop serves as classroom, theater, art-making space and container; fully dressed for events or used in its raw state for science or drop-in use. The Recycling Workshop and Grotto craft the lifelong lessons of careful use of resources, and encourage young artists and families to reclaim natural or discarded materials to find art, performance, and purpose.

BE PASSIONATE

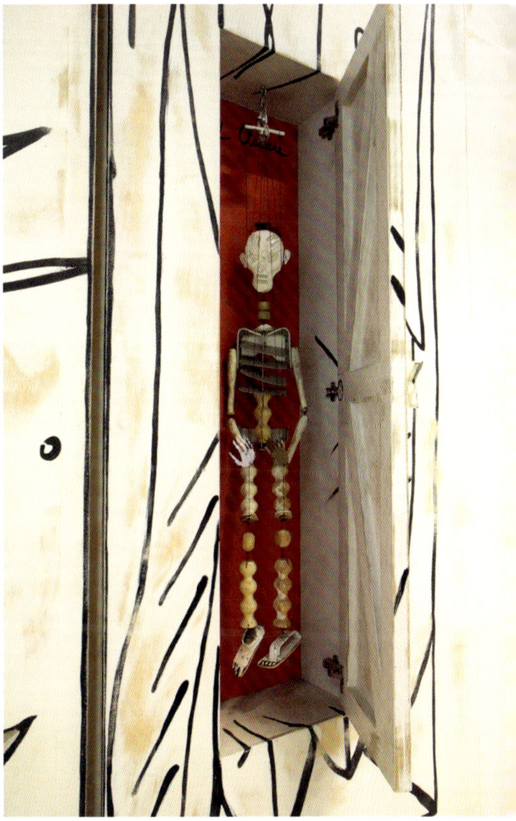

FROG PRINCE
PRINCE CHARMI

RUMPELSTILTSKIN
Sleep
BE PASSIONATE

DESIGNING TO BE HEARD

Rethinking what a multi-sensorial streetscape might be, we created STOMP as a museum experience filled with the potential to find beat, rhythm, and form in unexpected, non-traditional, found and often-discarded objects. Collaborating with the STOMP NY team, we built on the show's sense of exploration, performance, and of the unanticipated to energize a black box theater set within a museum setting. We used authentic stage-set backdrops alongside video of the world-famous touring ensemble to inspire and ignite imaginations. STOMP is the exploration of rhythm in everyday things; this is the space where these things can be found. Families make recycled instruments to bang on, rattle, shake and roll; they shoot baskets; mosaic a chain-link fence with colored caps; and run, slide, and pound out the beat. They drum, harmoniously or offbeat.

STOMP is the place to participate, a place of loud expression and energy. As the creators often say, STOMP is what it is!

BUILDING A LAND OF IMAGINATIVE EARLY LEARNING

WonderSCAPES is an arts and play-based environment accompanying preschool dedicated to early childhood development. In a creative and poetic collaboration with artist DeLoss McGraw, we designed WonderSCAPES to nurture and celebrate a child's own role in learning and in mastering their environment.

In a composition of murals, pattern, and poetry, WonderSCAPES encourages young children to traverse artistic and exploratory domains contributing to learning and literacy. *Alice's Pool* builds vocabulary in a mosaic water exhibit; *The March Hare's House & Tea Party* convey the concept of scale; and *Alice's Reading Forest* provides a soft-sculptured area for parents and children to socialize and share stories.

These flexible environments optimize programming, together acting as budding artist studio, accredited preschool, summer camp, and, on weekends, the WonderSCAPES birthday party room. A magical aesthetic inspired by *Alice's Adventures in Wonderland* aptly lends its themes of curiosity and discovery to the growth and identity of a child. WonderSCAPES is where imagination begins for the youngest of museum-goers.

NO ROOM
NO ROOM

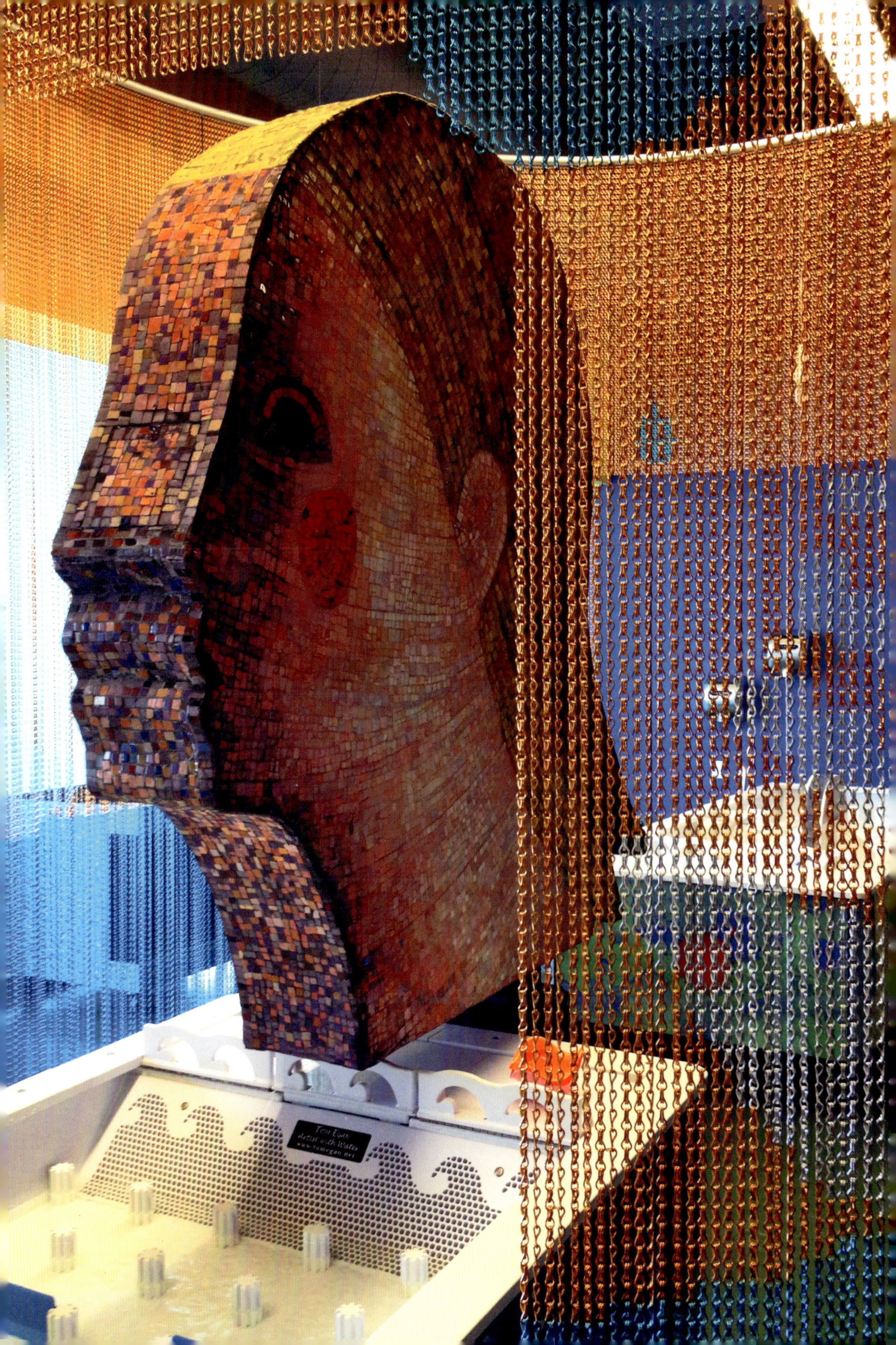
Tom Egan
Artist with Water
www.tomegan.net

MAKING ART ON CAMPUS ACCESSIBLE

Evocative art installations, contemporary millwork, and technology-enhanced design on a modest budget transform a family gallery in a sophisticated museum into a place of interactivity and beauty, one in which museum-goers of all ages are encouraged to be expressive and responsible through the act of making.

Our design program and envisioning process with the museum prioritized that the renovated gallery reach out to the university and community. We used artwork and a branded inglenook in which visitors can curl up to designate the gallery entry, making it visible from the campus commons. Removing all interior partitions made room for commissioned art installations, which pop into the all-white foreground, adding color, form, and content. An undulating frosty white table is positioned atop a blue landing strip flowing throughout the gallery as a clear, clean line of interactivity and art-making. Enhancing the social atmosphere, this continuous form offers enclaves for face-to-face encounters and opportunities for creative expression.

Our responsible and artful approach to the 750-square-foot renovation strategically reused embodied energies of existing walls, ceilings, and infrastructure; carpeting of 80 percent recycled fishing-net content; and LEDs and UV filters to retrofit track lighting, effectively lowering temperature, humidity, and glare. Special features include an irresistible touch-sensitive bench whose eighty LEDs emit responsive patterns, and the Cracking Art Group's recycled plastic *Blue Alligator* that extends artful experiences into the sculpture park. This cool gallery connects visitors of all ages to art, the Patricia & Phillip Frost Art Museum, and the Florida International University campus using traditional and technological methods of art-making and revealing the beauty of sustainable strategies.

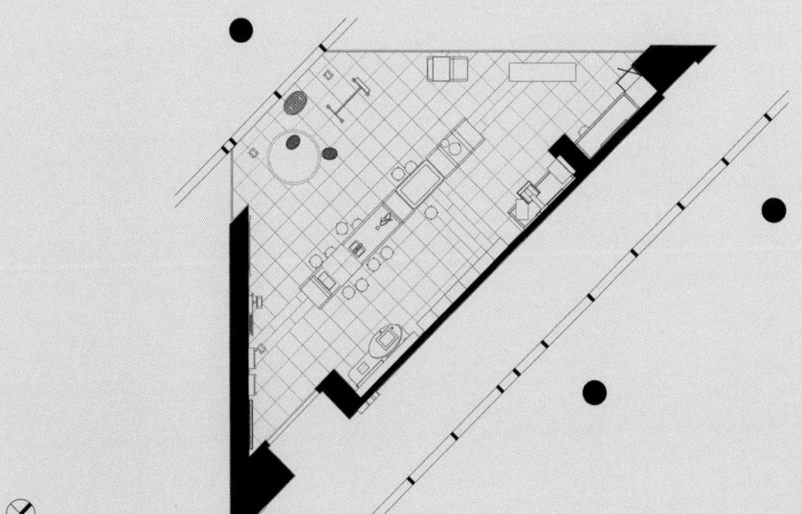

EXIT

GET INTO ART
PEOPLE
DISCOVER GREAT ART AND CREATE YOUR OWN!
The art book for children Yellow book
Kids

Picture me

SHARING MARITIME STORIES EXTENDS VISITOR ENGAGEMENT

St. Augustine Lighthouse & Maritime Museum keeps the stories of our nation's oldest port alive. Our approach to defying the traditional aligned with the desires of the museum and its executive director to break boring rules for historic site exhibits. Through architecture and storytelling, we supported the transformation of a disparate site into an interconnected campus of authentic play and preservation experiences that helps extend visitor engagement from 55 to 90 minutes.

Storytelling guides, rendered as cutout steel silhouettes of former lighthouse keepers and their families, and short stories give voice and presence to the lighthouse's histories, connecting museum-goers from one experience to the next. To help make the lighthouse more than just a 219-step climb, we added super-tall silhouette floor-spanning personages to add impact to the historic interior. Once-cluttered landings are now interactive places of respite. The characters punctuate lighthouse beauty and function, count steps, call out views, and engage via social media tools.

Within the adjacent Education Center, model ships share stories of famous Florida coastal journeys, and a miniature lighthouse permits accessible play and a scientific lens experiment.

Visitors previously intent on only the lighthouse climb are now attracted to the immersive experiences of the historic two-story keeper's home envisioned as a discovery lab and, submerging below, an interpretive undulating terrain of oceanographic topography.

1871

IMPACT HERE FOR CENTURIES.
KATE HARN
BECAME SECOND ASSISTANT KEEPER IN 1889, AT A SALARY OF $400 A YEAR, AFTER HER HUSBAND, HEAD KEEPER WILLIAM HARN PASSED AWAY IN THE KEEPERS' HOUSE OF TUBERCULOSIS.
165 FEET
HIGH
WHAT BIRDS DID YOU SEE AT THE TOP OF THE TOWER?
1980 16 WOMEN OF THE JUNIOR SERVICE LEAGUE SAVED THE LIGHT STATION BY TURNING BACK THE BULLDOZERS SENT TO DEMOLISH THE KEEPERS' HOUSE. THESE VOLUNTEERS HAD TO BE VERY DETERMINED TO SAVE THE HOUSE, TOWER AND FRESNEL LENS. IT TOOK THEM 15 YEARS AND $1.2 MILLION.

ONE MILLION BRICKS
HAVE YOU EVER FELT
STEPS
40
SECONDS
AT ONE TIME, ANASTASIA ISLAND WAS COVERED IN FLOCKS OF MIGRATING BIRDS WHO BECAME CONFUSED BY THE BRIGHT LIGHT AND OFTEN DASHED THEMSELVES AGAINST THE LIGHTHOUSE LANTERN.
HEAD KEEPER WILLIAM HARN USED HIS HAT TO PROTECT HIS FACE FROM "THOUSANDS OF WINGS".
ASSISTANT KEEPER DAVID SWAIN HUNTED THESE BIRDS IN THE 1930S, WHEN TURKEYS LIVED ON ANASTASIA ISLAND
WHY DO YOU THINK THERE ARE FEWER BIRDS HERE TODAY?
1980 16 WOMEN OF THE JUNIOR SERVICE LEAGUE SAVED THE LIGHT STATION BY TURNING BACK THE BULLDOZERS SENT TO DEMOLISH THE KEEPERS' HOUSE. THESE VOLUNTEERS HAD TO BE VERY DETERMINED TO SAVE THE HOUSE, TOWER AND FRESNEL LENS. IT TOOK THEM 15 YEARS AND $1.2 MILLION.

ST. AUGUSTINE LIGHTHOUSE KEEPER JOSEPH ANDREU FELL TO HIS DEATH WHILE HE WAS PAINTING THE FIRST ST. AUGUSTINE TOWER IN 1859. HIS WIFE MARIA DE LOS DELORES MESTRE BECAME THE FIRST HISPANIC WOMAN TO SERVE AS A LIGHT KEEPER IN THE UNITED STATES.
IN 1862, A PRISON BOAT SAT IN ST. AUGUSTINE HARBOR. LOCKED ABOARD WAS PAUL ARNAU, CONFEDERATE SYMPATHIZER, & THE COLLECTOR OF CUSTOMS FOR THE PORT OF ST. AUGUSTINE. ARNAU WAS HELD UNTIL HE REVEALED THE LOCATION OF THE FRESNEL LENS, AND THE LIGHTHOUSE CLOCKWORKS THAT HAD BEEN HIDDEN IN THE COUNTRYSIDE THE YEAR BEFORE.
MARCH 31
1936
ELECTRICITY IS USED FOR THE FIRST TIME IN THE LIGHTHOUSE LENS. THE GLOW OF THE LENS CHANGED FROM THE YELLOW OF A KEROSENE LAMP TO THE WHITE OF ELECTRICITY
LIGHTHOUSE LEGENDS
#PLUGGINGIN
KATE CORY
HMS PANDORA

USCGC FIR
CLOUD

MAKING ARCHAEOLOGY FUN

WRECKED shares St. Augustine's Lighthouse & Maritime Museum's shipwreck stories and colonial currents through archaeological lenses. We sensitively and sustainably inserted a contemporary salon within the historic lighthouse keeper's home to create an object-based immersive environment.

In juxtaposition to the Victorian parlor, we defined a modern portal to welcome visitors, defined by its crisply drafted and authentic archaeological grid. These one-meter marks denote geographical and historical points of interest as interpretive elements flowing throughout the salon. A timeline brings a cast of characters to the surface: yesterday's sailors, Loyalist refugees, today's archaeologists, and tomorrow's explorer, *Star Waters*, a comic-book character and youthful purveyor of revolutionary shipwrecks.

The salon features holographic wallpaper and polycarbonate chandeliers using Fresnel optics of lighthouses to highlight views that make the watchtower a focus of exploration. The fireplace wall grid and graphic viewport impart shipwreck discoveries via digital and analog experiences. We designed the furnishings to reference maritime building techniques and materiality, including the lighthouse daymark appearing as a signature striped tabletop. Ancillary learning stations feature hands-on navigation tools and digital gaming to dive and recover artifacts.

The WRECKED salon further extends visitor engagement beyond that of the lighthouse itself.

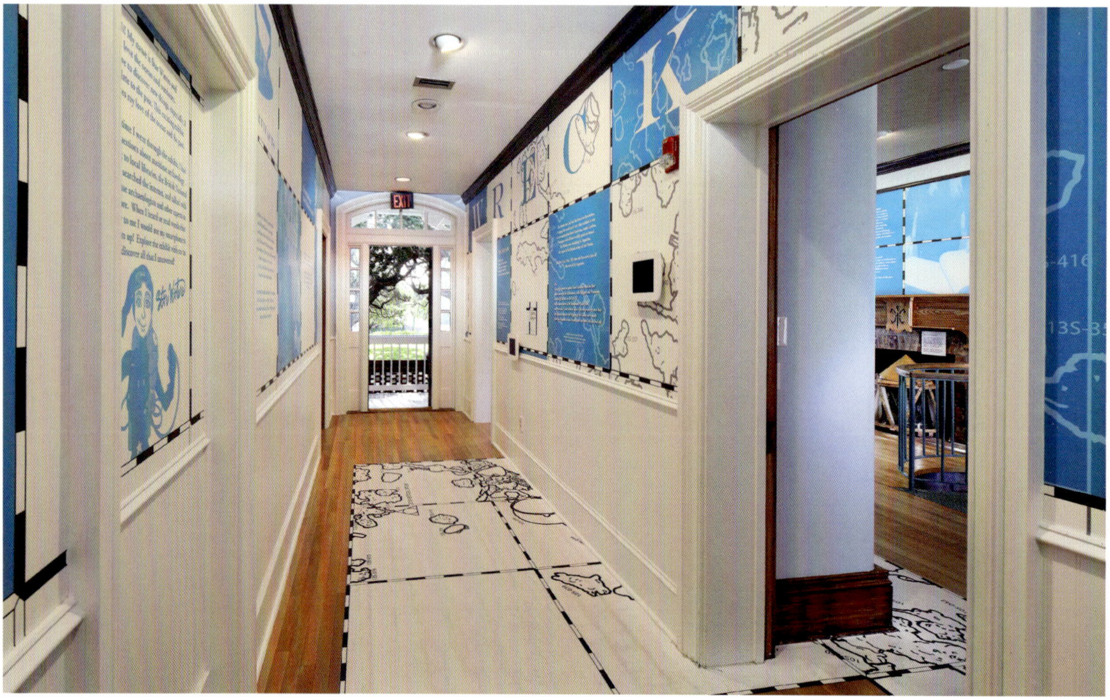

DONORS
Thank you to the
Lastinger Family Foundation
for their generous support to
make possible WRECKED,
an interactive, educational exhibition.

Not only do Lighthouse archaeologists
survey the ocean floor, they survey historical archives
and study documents for information about artifacts,
shipping, events, and circumstances of the time period.
Our research at the British National Archives revealed
details about the evacuation of Charleston,
including names of ships, number of people leaving,
and which British regiments where involved.
Military uniform buttons found on the shipwreck belong
only to those regiments listed as part of the evacuation of Charleston,
providing one of the strongest links to the loyalist evacuation.
Though historical documents tell us much
about military maneuvers, ships cargos and similar types of information,
they share relatively little about the everyday lives of soldiers and sailors.
Their clothing, household goods, weapons and cookery
recovered from the shipwreck tell a very different story
than that told in historical documents.
Exploring both in this exhibit gives us a broader view of the past.
DRUM LENS

LEAVING CHARLESTON
HIDE & SEEK

SCULPTING A SANDBAR TO CHALLENGE CURIOSITY

Submerging into the basement of the lighthouse keeper's home, museum-goers embark upon the WRECKED sandbar as an immersive journey. Visitors traverse the sandbar's fluid form to learn about the perilous St. Augustine coastline from the museum's sunken archaeological finds. Artifacts situated within the symbolic sandbar show and tell stories, through one-meter-gridded overlays representing the actual dive. The modular sandbar floats lightly on steel frames, raised slightly for moisture management, and supports larger artifacts, like a 770-pound iron cannon rescued from the 1780's wreck. As the sandbar flows, it extends to form object nooks and bench displays, leaving the historic structure untouched.

Object outposts flowing up from the sandbar delicately lean without fasteners on the fragile coquina walls protecting historic integrity, demonstrating maritime construction techniques, and highlighting recovered treasures, from the smallest pewter military button to the ship's heavy bell.

To connect museum-goers to stories of naval archaeology, geology, and sustainability, we sourced salvaged wormwood, once submerged for seventy-five years, to construct the sandbar. Its natural beauty warms the bare twin basement halls and the brick cistern. We designed the WRECKED sandbar to serve as sculpture, interpretive device, floating classroom, and object of curiosity.

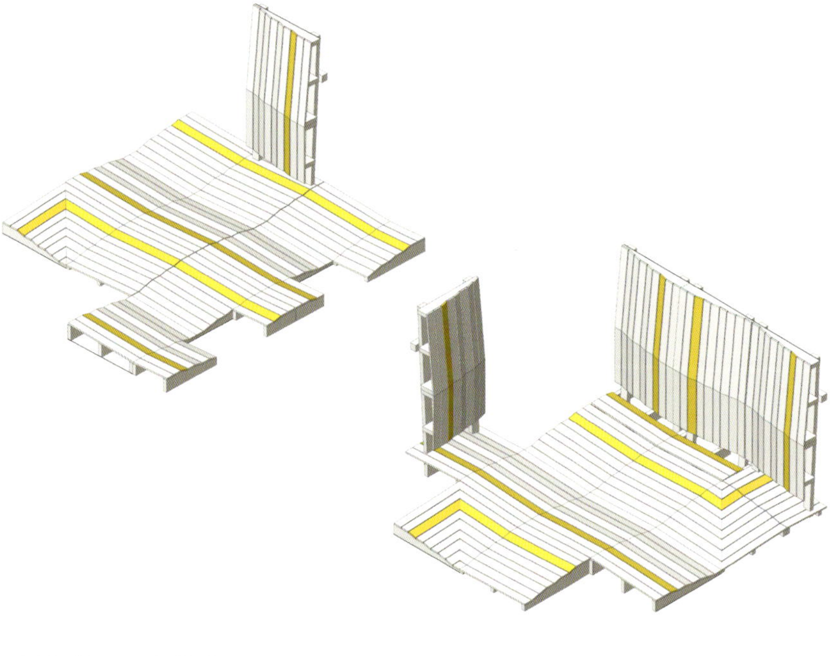

OPENING DOORS TO LEARNING

By building a vibrant home for a children's museum in an abandoned retail warehouse, we demonstrate an important philosophical message of value. Transformed from an obsolete commercial structure into a welcoming civic symbol and a safe environment for play and learning, DuPage Children's Museum practices what it preaches.

We took great care and thought with the museum's architecture, resilience, imagery, and playfulness. Recycled into something extraordinary, the building architecture uses iconographic elements children understand and appreciate. Our *Big Red Door* welcomes everyone and has become the museum's identity, emblematic of what the museum stands for: opening doors for children to learning. The building and its integrated exhibits were a factor in attendance doubling the first year, rising to over 300,000 visitors annually.

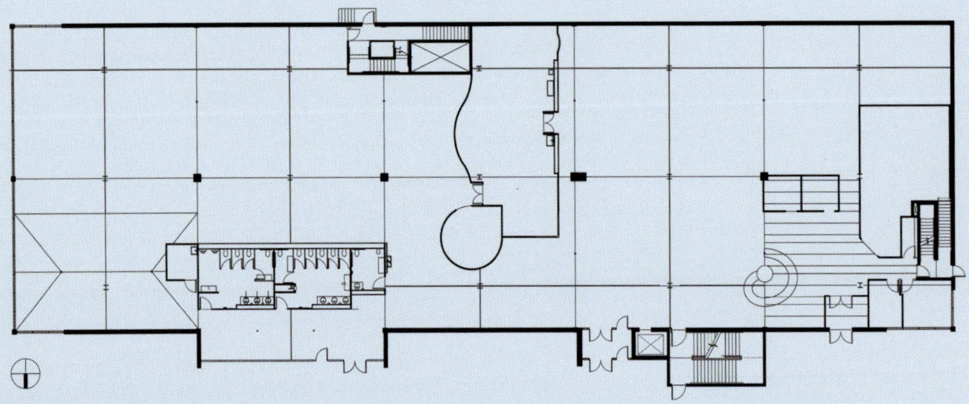

Children's
MUSEUM

RESTORING IN CHILDREN'S TERMS

Sixteen years after our initial design, burst pipes caused massive flood damage to all three floors of the 42,000-square-foot museum. With insurance and schedule as key restoration challenges, we brought familiarity with the complicated building and an understanding of the museum's hands-on approach to learning that were essential to meet opening day, a mere six months later.

While initial construction stages, from mold remediation to addressing structural integrity, were in play, we expressed the museum's brand as elements inspiring creativity, sustainability, and invention. A few salvageable original items, including the well-loved fishing boat and birthday zones, were turned over to artists for re-imaging. By re-addressing staff needs, a round office became the evocative *Wonder Room*, a site-specific artist installation exploring technology, color, and active learning. The new *Pyramid Bench* embraces the public space as a portal, connecting family engagement and play in ways that transition visitors from the entry into creative galleries. The *Big Lawn* is a visually appealing space for kids to experiment with movement. The ramp and hills fit together, so that we could incorporate an accessible compatible experience seamlessly and with delight.

Designing at high speed, accepting risk, and staying true to the original led to resilient and expedited solutions, all facilitated by our design team, the museum, local politicians, business community, and 1,000 volunteers. Recognized as a national leader among early learning facilities, DuPage Children's Museum's reputation for being innovative transformed the enormity of the restoration project into opportunities to restore the museum in children's terms. Our thoughtful architecture brands the museum's unique learning experiences by re-imagining the interior as a healthy and responsible environment

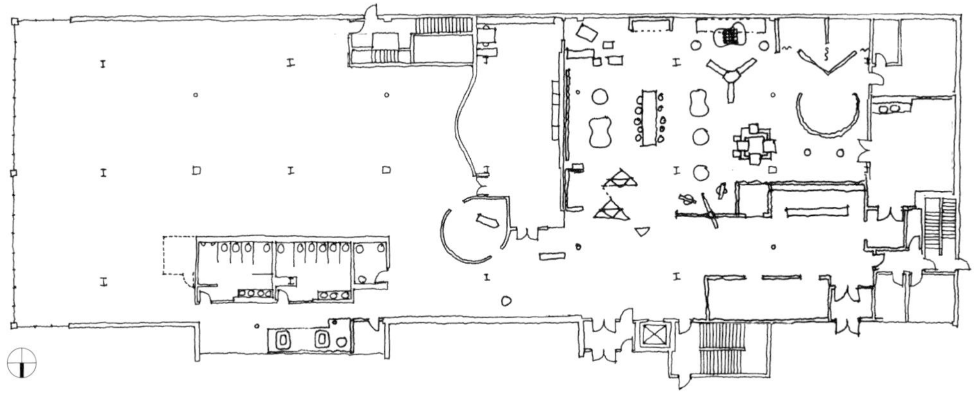

You can

CREATIVITY CONNECTIONS
Creativity is thinking BIG!

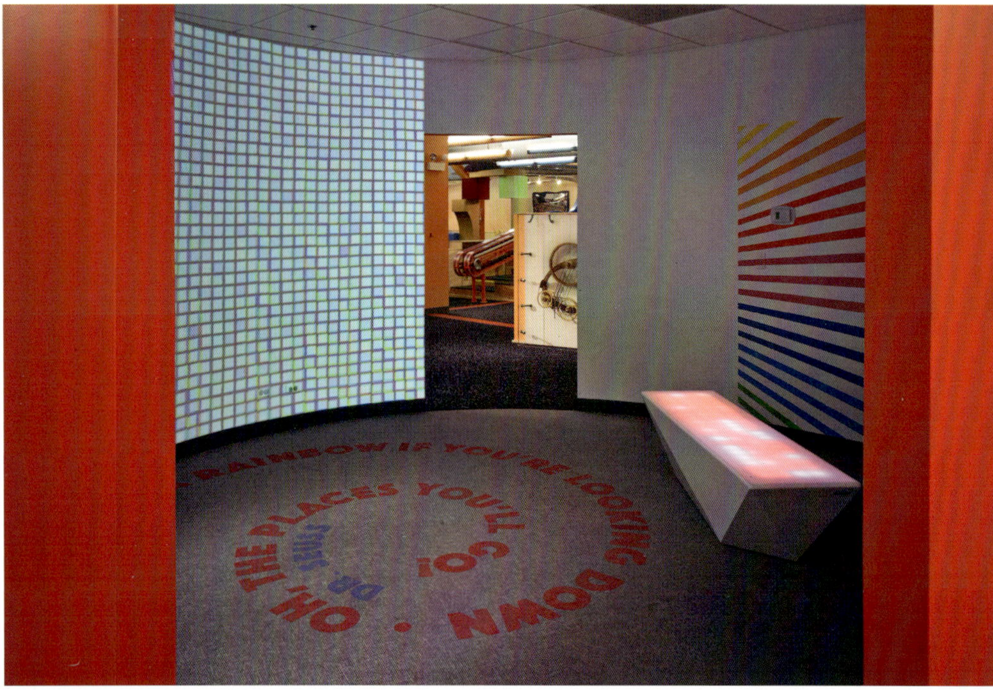
RAINBOW IF YOU'RE LOOKING DOWN
OH, THE PLACES YOU'LL GO!
DR. SEUSS

CULTIVATING COMMUNITY ON THE FARM

As a community hub and center for intergenerational interactions, the Exploration Station fuses nature and community purpose.

When entrusted with the design of Exploration Station, we paid homage to its agrarian site, while creatively transforming it. Set on the historic 170-acre Perry Farm, an ad-hoc collection of barn structures is familiar yet surprising, sophisticated yet sweet. The museum's iconic entry is a billboard of high-octane stripes, identifiable by kids and recognizable by the community as a safe, fun place to explore. We played with the details: a striped concrete path, yellow open-air silo, and cutout entry desk, which lead into the 10,000-square-foot museum; all offering ample room for groups to gather. Our "Lucky Charm" windows of rectangles, triangles, and half-moons cast alluring patterns of natural light on the interior and lead to the exhibit galleries beyond. One opening is purposely high, suggesting the youngest of visitors be lifted up to peek out.

The Exploration Station serves over 50,000 visitors and creates a multi-million-dollar economic impact annually on its tri-city area.

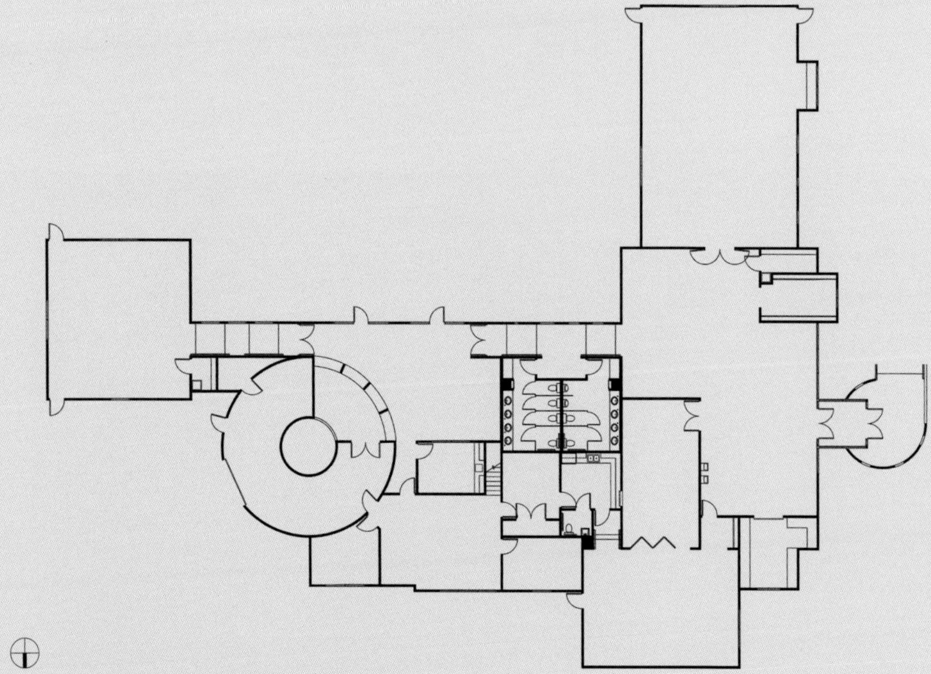

INSPIRING COMMUNITY TO IMPROVE DOWNTOWN

Architecture can be communal. In Saginaw, Michigan, a community the automotive industry left behind, our transformation of a discarded car dealership into a vibrant children's museum reinforces architecture's role as a community-connector and catalyst for revitalization. Recycled into an extraordinary destination, immersive interiors use iconographic elements that children understand and appreciate. *Big Kids* welcome everyone and are emblematic of the museum's mission: celebrating reuse and bringing three neighboring communities together to play and learn.

Big Kids direct children to relevant themes, such as healthcare and those of regional significance, aiming to spark industry through collaboration and innovation. We collaborated with regional school districts to connect exhibits with curriculum and worked with an experienced local contractor to deliver a project big on design at half the typical build-out costs.

We believe interactive architecture is a vital investment in community; our design attracts over 100,000 visitors each year, supporting downtown revitalization.

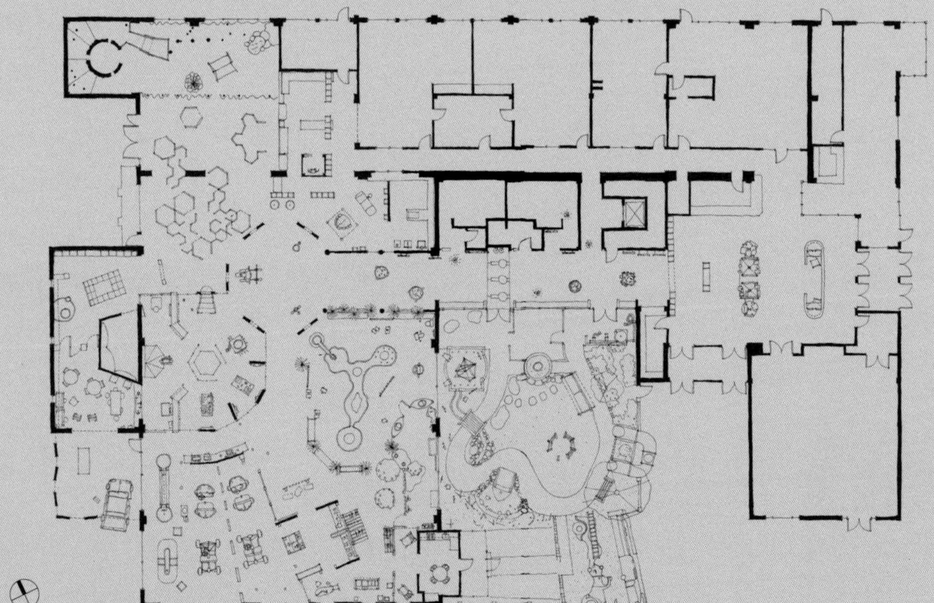

hopedic
geon's
ffice

Try It!

CONNECTING LITERATURE AND NATURE

Our flowing design for the children's library shifted it radically from its previous formality, yet takes its inspiration from the main library's Prairie-based architectural style. Breaking from rigidity, this accessible environment has ample room for families to make literary and social discoveries, meander, and find their place.

Within an imaginative landscape, a pink ribbon of quotes floats overhead while a commissioned mosaic fountain, the *KinderSpring*, provides a warm welcome to the Children's Library and Reading Gardens. The *KinderSpring* entertains and educates with sensor-controlled sounds and a sustainable spray of color-changing fiber optics. *Mac's Garden* is a quiet and sheltered garden for infant and toddler exploration. Preschoolers plant alphabet flowers at the *Garden Gates*, and test keys that open *Discovery Boxes*. School-age children find their spot in the *Art Gardens* with troughs full of raw constructive materials, reminiscent of revered desks from Frank Lloyd Wright's Johnson Wax building. The fanciful elements, referencing nature, shift scale from low and petite to giant and oversized. Soaring *Trees*, enticing developmentally appropriate niches, ingenious materials, and furnishings reuse create character while resulting in less than 23 percent of demolished material being removed from site.

Increased attendance and popularity have proven that this ever-changing garden of literary delights, with imagery based on art and books found in the stacks, is irresistible to children and their families.

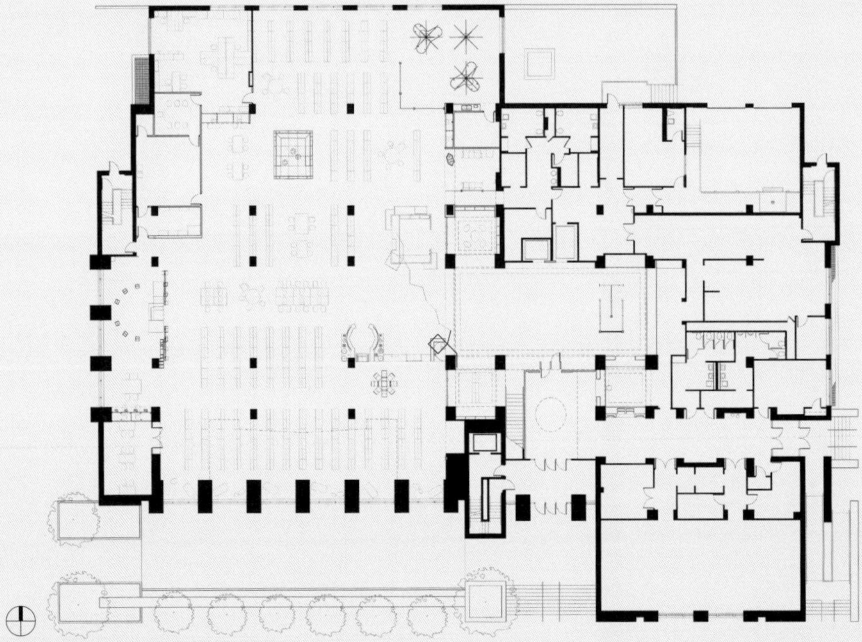

There is more treasure in books
than in all the pirate's loot
ne more that you read,
the more things you will know.
If a book is really good,
it deserves to be read again.
a good library...
I have found the best way
and then advice

Baby Food

DESIGNING WITH ATTITUDE SERVES TEENS

Teens are very often the first to admit that they have conflicting needs, which was reflected by their request for physical separation from the main library. We translated the young adult advisory panel's desire for their own distinct space. Re-working a floor plan of the Evanston Public Library, we carved 2,000 square feet out of outdated media space that has easy access to staff and adult reference materials, ensuring that separation did not equate as isolation.

A storefront-like entry with illuminated digital letters, set within a translucent honeycomb panel, spells out ownership. A palette expressive of the teens' sophisticated ideas evolved presenting a formal-informal duality. A serious side featuring computers, study carrels, and task lighting is countered by the silly side where teens chill out in an egg chair and lounge under mod lights. A glitch of wallpapers speaks of encryption indicative of teen communicative habits and inspired by text and technology. The *Reading Bar*, a café-inspired counter, surrounds the wall of monitors and informal stage that the teens or the teen librarian operate for improv, poetry slams, or performance. The Loft carves out room and resource for a previously underserved group of library users.

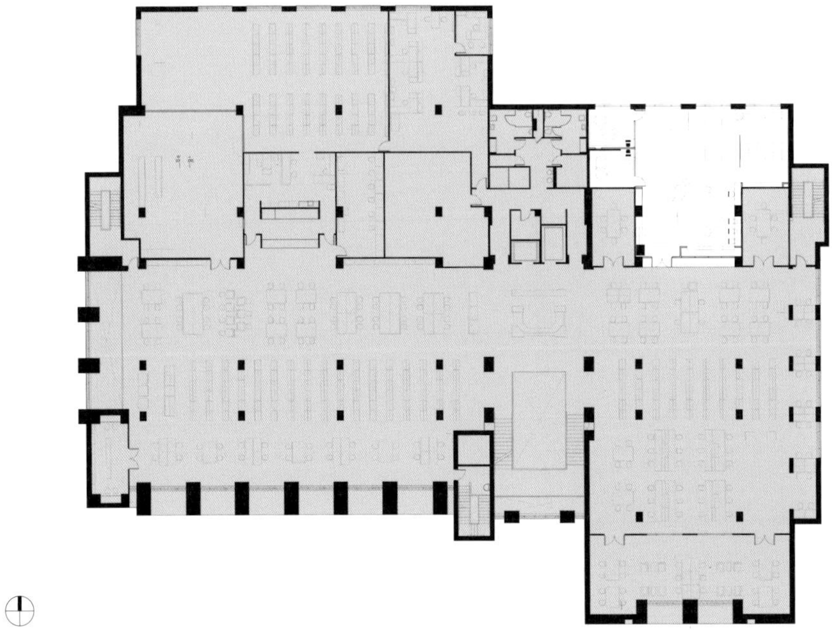

ATTRACTING TEENS THROUGH EQUITABLE DESIGN

The Vortex, named by the young adults it attracts, is a distinct and distinctive space and a microcosm of the "real adult" Fountaindale Public Library. We provided an identity that speaks to teen interests and aesthetics: moments of surprise and juxtaposition, from a large beckoning anime wall-wrap announcing the computer "bar," to the commissioned "Think Epic" art chain drape and branded entry. Low, plush two-sided seating can be reconfigured by teens to face the performance area or lean towards the digital consoles.

The Vortex is a social catalyst for teens hungry for increased casual interactions in a digital age. We super-sized hefty wood tables to function as a communal feast of face-to-face time. Situated under eye-popping origami lights, the XL tables became the library's methodology for employing a real social network and generating a welcoming, comfortable atmosphere where teens find their place.

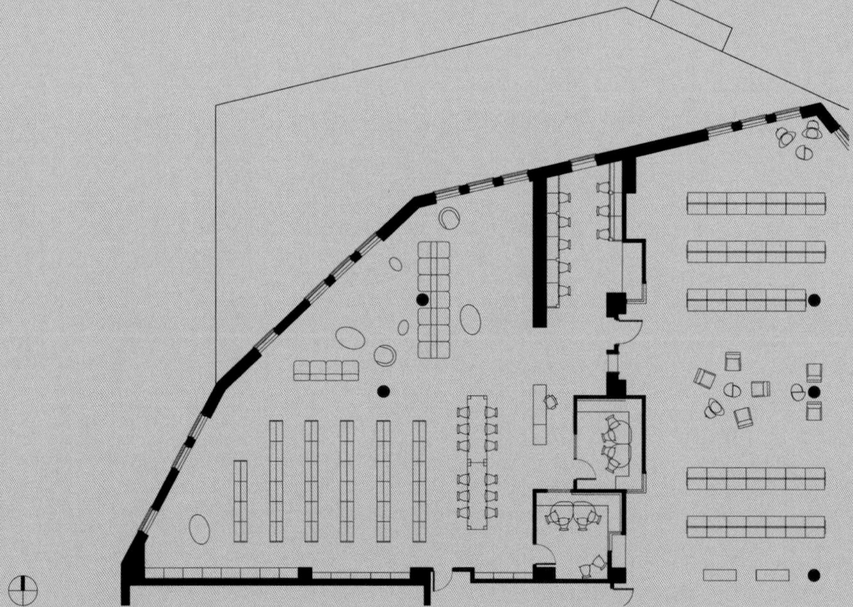

PLANTING A FOREST OF LITERATURE AND PLAY

Our *Dragon Trees*, planted in the children's library, become icons and signifiers welcoming the highly diverse community whose families frequent the library. We brought one of the librarian's favorite storytime books (by Jane Langton) to life in a forest of adventure. Soaring tree canopies entice children to a landscape where art and story come alive, and where familiarity enriches a sense of place and purpose.

The entry Dragon Tree introduces a structural vocabulary of flexibility and diversity. Each tree is individual, planting distinct interactive opportunities for play under outstretched canopies or hanging objects that change with the seasons or art-making, from its branches. Quotations from favorite librarian stories are embroidered onto the stylized tree panels. Children are drawn to the trees as distinct nodes of learning and creativity: the *Entry Tree* that displays daily activities; the *Secret Garden* canopy with microscopic views of nature; the *Creativity Park Tree*; *Think Park Study Rooms*; and *Computer Park*. Children delight in finding the *World Park Tree* near the different language books, and where they can play games known around the world. We created multiple perimeter nooks to nestle up under tiered windows, which cast natural light and shadows through the tree branches. Some may notice that the Dragon Tree frames resemble the stainless-steel bases of the Eames Eiffel chair, a deliberate connection to a clean and modern aesthetic.

Creating vistas within the library, the *Dragon Trees* nurture the literature-rich landscape in which children discover a variety of spaces to learn, play, and read.

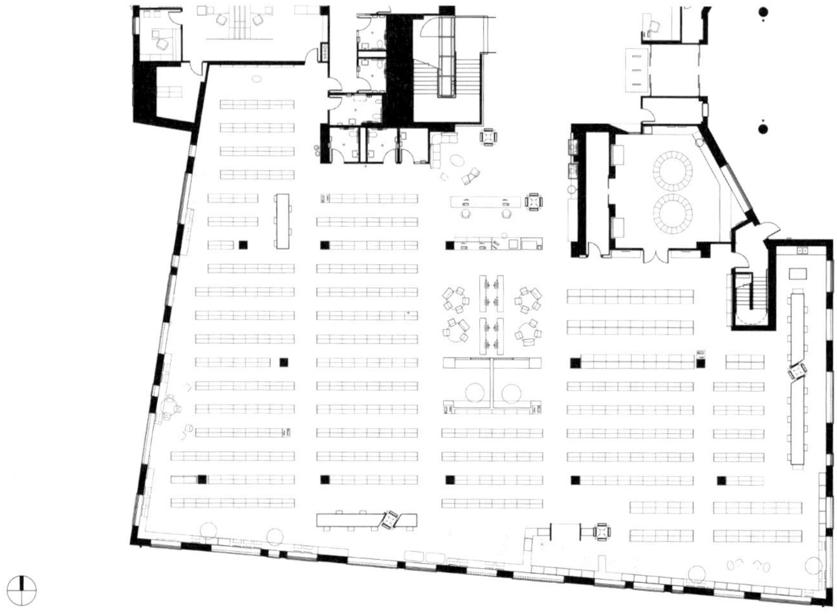

I LOVE YOU RIGHT UP TO THE MOON AND BACK

can't keep still all day
I LIKE ADVENTURES
and i'm going to find one

I LOVE YOU RIGHT UP TO THE MOON AND BACK

EXIT

MIGHTY OAK
was once a
like you
The Coral Reef

IVERSITY
Creatures Of The World
Wilson
cier Bay, Alaska

RECRUITING NEXT-GENERATION LEARNERS WITH LOFTY SPACE

A glorious gateway to elementary education at St. Chrysostom's Day School, this small project demonstrates how 685 square feet of space was transformed into a relevant and inspiring place for learning and play. In service seven days a week for the day school, the nursery, and even adult programs, the former 1893 chapel needed renovation, access, egress, and system enhancements.

Tracery, arches, and peek-a-boo quatrefoils build upon the historic church's Gothic sensibilities. The loft play space and verticality of a cathedral of Tinkertoy-like trees reinforce spatial and spiritual awareness, while creating canopied objects for exploration. The loft features wide stairs doubling as seating and a performance proscenium. Controllable LED color-changing lights provide theatricality and interactive wall panels develop fine motor and perception skills. Inviting seating for caregivers at child-height encourages shared experience. When the treehouse becomes a backdrop, toy cabinets fold away and the space transforms and tidies for adult education in the off hours.

We designed a "play sandwich" that places resource and storage at one end, activity and clean-up at the other, with a "filling" of centers for messy art making and creative play. To meet an aggressive twelve-week schedule and budget constraints, custom millwork is balanced alongside affordable school furniture with intelligent built-in storage. A clever swap-out of variously stained wood cabinet doors adds charm. Candlestick-like light fixtures familiar to churchgoers, responsible flooring, and energy-efficient fans ensure the space is comfortable, user-controlled, and operationally viable. The Treehouse Chapel is an uplifting, friendly, and soaring reuse of architecture that has also become the first place on tours for church and school recruitment.

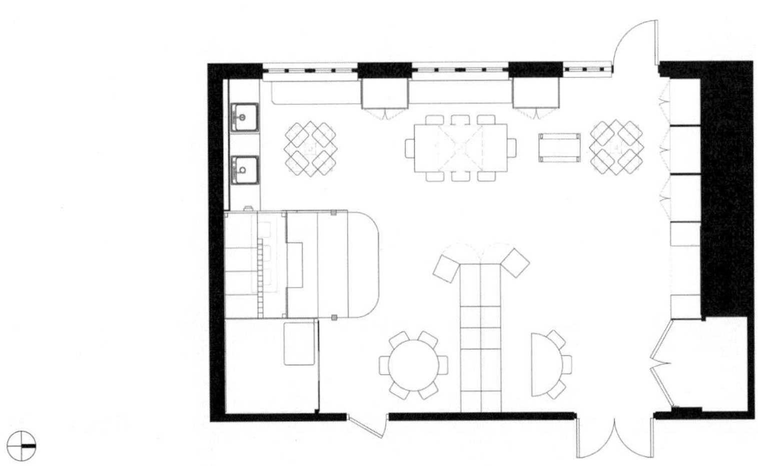

Winter
SNOWY DAY
Snow Bunny Tales

PLANTING SEEDS OF INSPIRATIONAL PLAY

We converted an urban back alley into an uplifting 450-square-foot Gothic Garden. This cathedral of trees is a place of inspiration, creativity, and sanctuary designed for children at play in the out-of-doors. Soaring arches, reaching up to embrace the sky, articulate a purposeful space that feels larger than its physical boundaries. The alley is adorned with art making; the fire stair becomes a performance hall; and lofty vaulted canopies resonate with artful wind chimes and playful gizmos.

Our architecture, with its tracery, arches, vaults, peek-a-boo quatrefoil cutouts, and modular grid, establishes its functional importance as an endearing landscape for reflection, seeing, storytelling, gardening, and exploration, while building upon the historic church's gothic sensibilities and emotive beauty. One supporter was so inspired by the transformation to a garden, she became a leading donor to the school's mission.

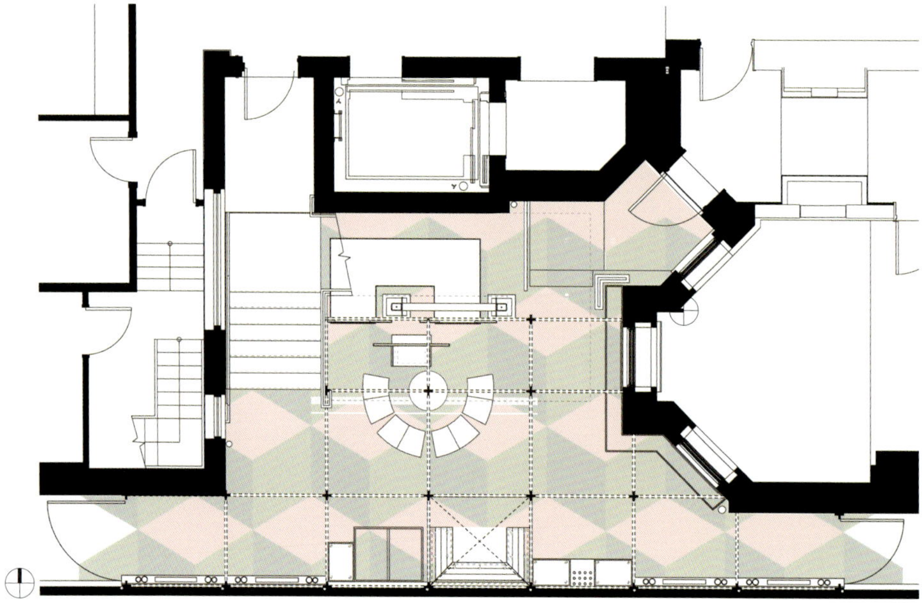

MAKING PEDIATRIC VISITS HAPPIER

An entrepreneurial pediatrician's mantra to be "Pixar-like" challenged us to create an inviting medical office embedded with forward-thinking strategies; one that supports new approaches and technologies to meet a growing healthcare market. Our design makes staff visible, orientation obvious, and branding informative and accessible; this shapes the right impression and builds trust between patient and practice.

We focused on how interactivity and a clean aesthetic could create a welcoming, reassuring, and flexible environment that embeds the latest medical technologies and supports the needs of families. Expressing flexibility and accommodating caregiving, our super-sized welcome desk affords great staff visibility with room for remote patient monitoring and telehealth technology. Keeping mobile otoscopes and Polaroid cameras handy for playful patient snaps are part of creating this accessible and meaningful healthcare experience. Extra-wide storefront doors permit easy access. The adaptable waiting room suits wellness and sick visits, video conference parent orientation sessions, and evening classes.

We designed the millwork as a cabinet of curiosities, with sustainably harvested natural woods with water-based washes of calming color. A series of building block cubes and a Tinkertoy-like tree help keep the plethora of stuff (puzzles and patient artwork) uncluttered and close at hand. Each exam room projects its own cheerful identity. Our exam tables feature building block legs and easy-to-sanitize nanotechnology vinyl toppers; our sweetly surfaced infant measurers are the antithesis of typical pediatric furnishings.

Being Pixar-minded, we defined a replicable model that is both inventive and inviting, optimizing the accessibility of the pediatric practice and the support provided. Our client's network and reach has more than tripled; three new offices attest to how a well-designed, tech-enhanced, accessible, and relatable environment can meet a child's needs while supporting twenty-first century medical care—and beyond!

The Rocky Mountains

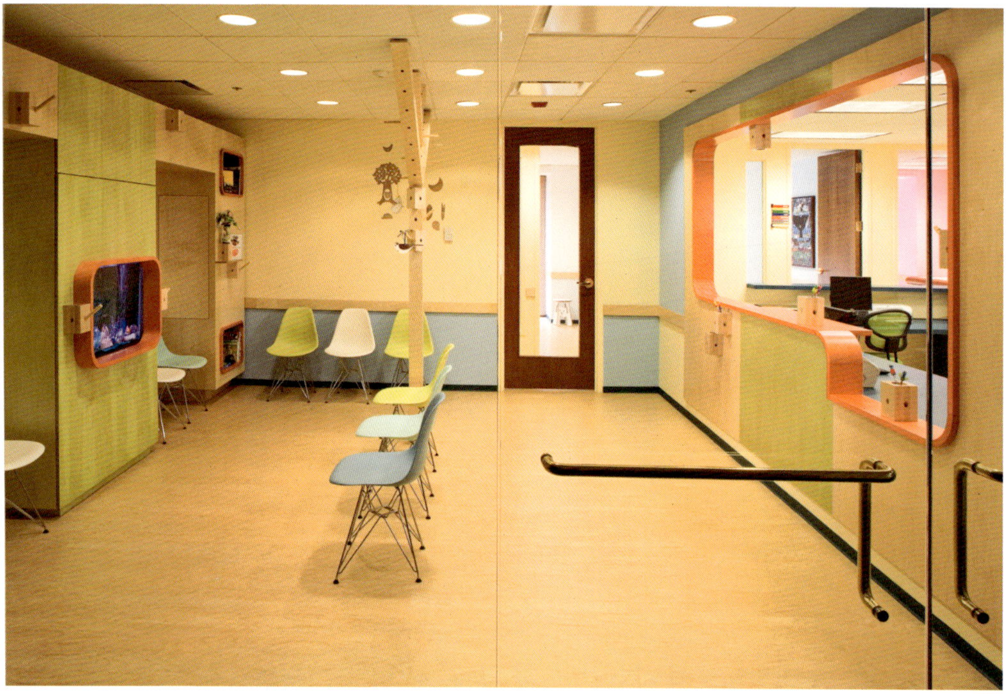

DESIGNING FUN FOR EVERYONE

Our playful aesthetic elevates everyday living and enhances fun, work, and learning spaces and places. Expanding our studio's advocacy for play and as a natural adjunct to architectural practice and process, we created affordable and accessible products that fuel a consciousness of design and beauty. Leveraging our long-standing relationships and custom collaborations with our industry partners, we are designing collections for living, work, and play.

We produce Studio Printworks wallpapers, linens, and draperies, plus our line of kids' furnishings and energy-producing hands-on play and learning elements. Born In Brooklyn features Happy Face stools and Happyland tables, theaters, and toy/book boxes that charm and fit nurseries, libraries, and residential buildings.

Designing products extends the reach of our practice and allows us to become makers of artful adventure, active discovery, and creative exploration—all hallmarks of memory-making experiences.

EXPERIENCES MATTER

Young At Art Museum | Cultural | Davie, Florida (see page 60)

Cave: Education Pavilion and Orientation Theater | Cultural | Young At Art Museum | Davie, Florida (see page 68)

Exploration Station | Cultural | Bourbonnais, Illinois (see page 114)

Frost Art Museum | Cultural | Frost Art Museum at Florida International University | Miami, Florida (see page 84)

Stinking Truth About Garbage | Educational | Chicago Children's Museum | Chicago, Illinois

Kids On The Fly | Civic Public Space | O'Hare International Airport | Chicago, Illinois

ArtSCAPES | Cultural | Young At Art Museum | Davie, Florida (see page 60)

Kenny Scharf's Closet | Cultural | Young At Art Museum | Davie, Florida (see page 60)

STOMP | Cultural | Young At Art Museum | Davie, Florida (see page 76)

Fountaindale Public Library | Cultural | Fountaindale, Illinois (see page 134)

St. Augustine Lighthouse & Maritime Museum | Cultural | St. Augustine, Florida (see pages 90, 96, 100)

Redline Virtual Reality | Entertainment | Hospitality | Chicago, Illinois

Cybercafé | Cultural | Educational | Alliance Française de Chicago | Chicago, Illinois

The Loft for Teens| Cultural | Evanston Public Library | Evanston, Illinois

Interactive Science Forum | Educational | The Latin School of Chicago | Chicago, Illinois (see page 54)

The Vortex | Cultural | Fountaindale Public Library | Bolingbrook, Illinois (see page 130)

Children's Library | Cultural | Evanston Public Library |
Evanston, Illinois (see page 122)

CultureSCAPES | Cultural | Educational | Young At Art Museum |
Davie, Florida (see page 60)

My Museum | Educational | Chicago Children's Museum | Chicago, Illinois

DuPage Children's Museum: Restoration | Cultural | Educational | DuPage Children's Museum | Naperville, Illinois (see page 108)

SPROUTS Laboratory | Cultural | Burpee Museum of Natural History | Rockford, Illinois

Garden in the City: The Children's Midway | Pop-up | The City of Chicago | Chicago, Illinois

DuPage Children's Museum | Cultural | Naperville, Illinois (see page 104)

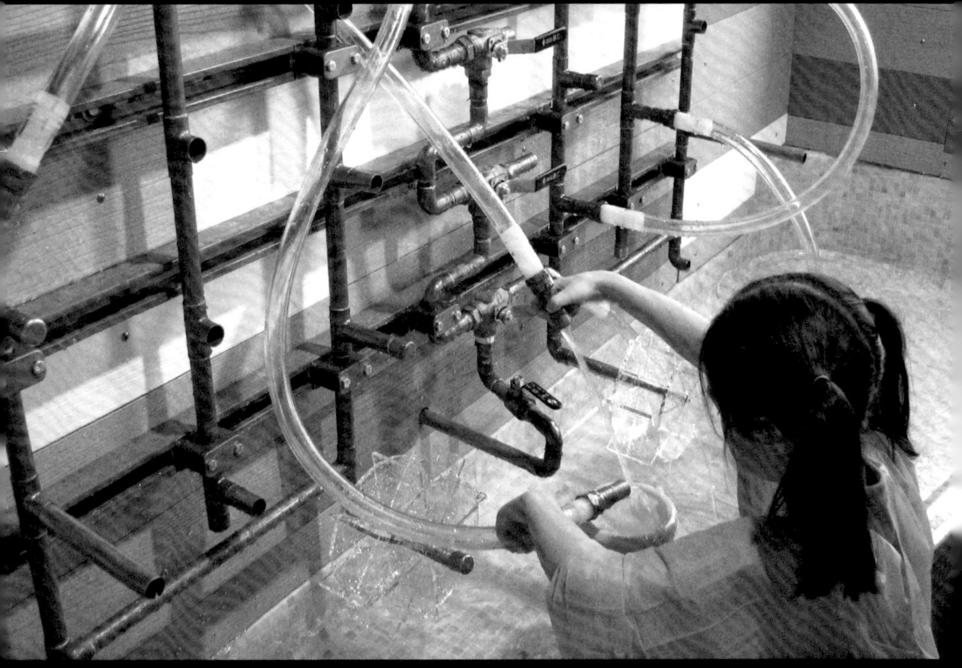

Splash | Educational | Louisville Science Museum | Louisville, Kentucky

Kidscommons | Cultural | Columbus Children's Museum | Columbus, Indiana

NatureSCAPES | Cultural | Educational | Young At Art Museum | Davie, Florida (see page 60)

Lincoln Park Zoo: Pritzker Family Children's Zoo | Civic Public Space | Chicago, Illinois (see page 48)

WIND | Cultural | Educational | DuPage Children's Museum | Naperville, Illinois (see page 104)

KidZone | Educational | Louisville Science Center | Louisville, Kentucky

Get FIT! | Recreational | Educational | Louisville Science Center |

Children's Museum of Fond du Lac | Cultural | Fond du Lac, Wisconsin

Children's Museum of Brownsville | Cultural | Brownsville, Texas

Swim School Prototype | Recreational | National Rollout, United States

Great Room | Residential | Private Client | Chicago, Illinois

Swim School Prototype | Recreational | National Rollout, United States

Lake Shore Drive Apartment | Residential | Private Client | Chicago, Illinois

Field Museum of Natural History | Cultural | Civic Public Space | Chicago, Illinois

Lincoln Park Zoo: Pritzker Family Children's Zoo | Civic Public Space | Chicago, Illinois (see page 48)

Field Museum of Natural History | Cultural | Civic Public Space | Chicago, Illinois

Lincoln Park Zoo: Pritzker Family Children's Zoo | Civic Public Space | Chicago, Illinois (see page 48)

Song of Korea | Cultural | Educational | Austin, Texas

WonderSCAPES | Cultural | Young At Art Museum | Davie, Florida (see page 78)

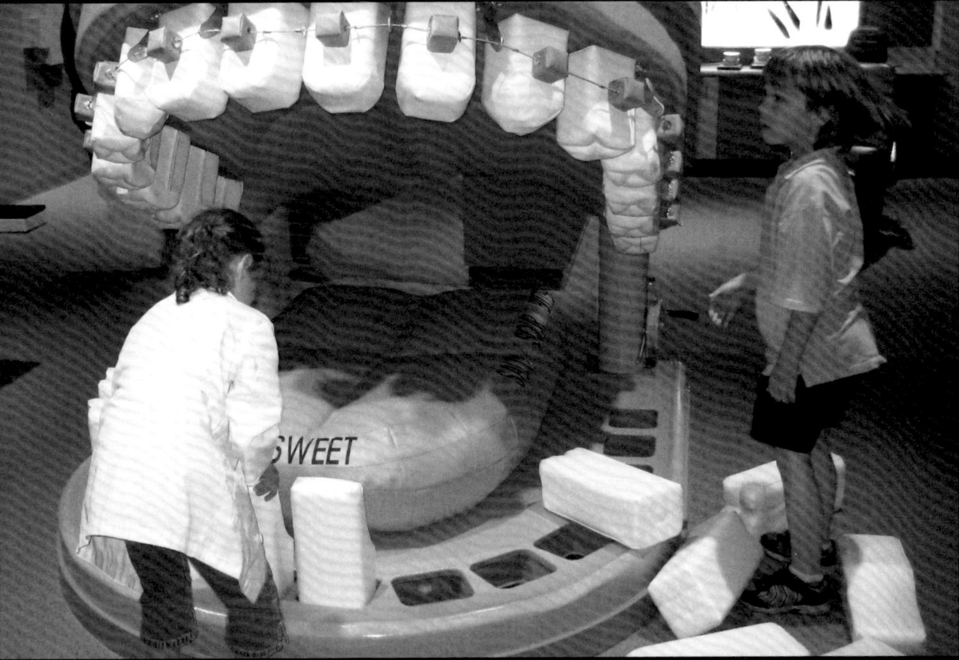

Mid-Michigan Children's Museum | Cultural | Educational | Saginaw, Michigan (see page 118)

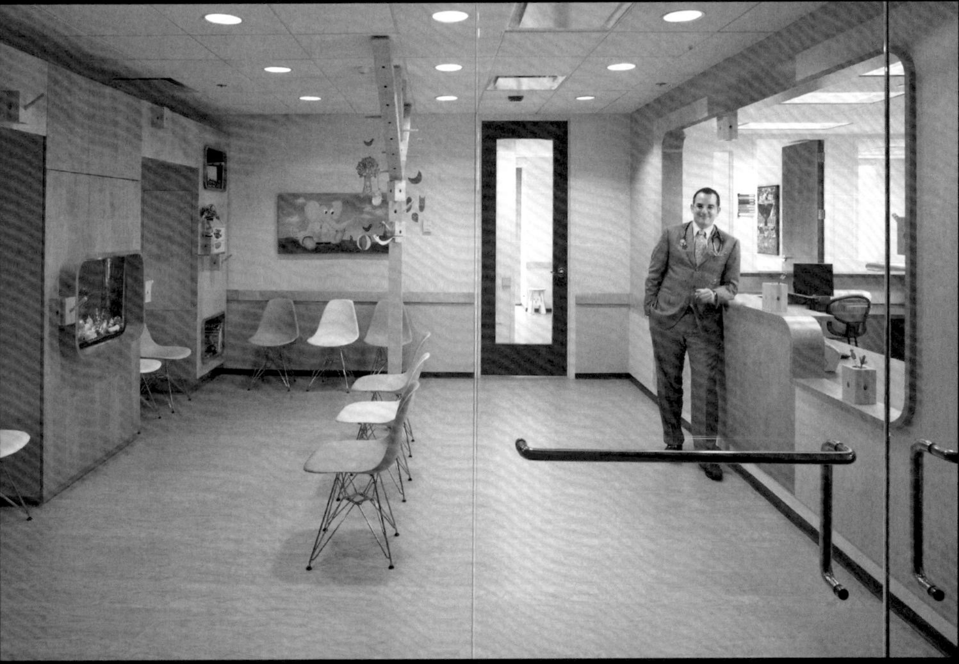

Pediatric Prototype | Healthcare | Chicago, Illinois (see page 150)

Chez Kids Academy | Cultural | Educational | Alliance Française de Chicago | Chicago, Illinois

Gothic Garden | Spiritual | Educational | St. Chrysostom's Day School | Chicago, Illinois (see page 146)

Granger Community Church | Spiritual | Educational | Granger, Indiana

Treehouse Chapel | Spiritual | Educational | St. Chrysostom's Day School | Chicago, Illinois (see page 140)

Bonner Heritage Farm | Landscape | Recreational | Lindenhurst, Illinois

Independence Grove | Landscape | Recreational | Libertyville, Illinois

Reggio Outdoor Learning Playground | Landscape | Recreational | Winnetka Public School Nursery | Winnetka, Illinois

Ronald McDonald House | Healthcare | Multifamily Residential | Oak Lawn, Illinois (see page 42)

ACKNOWLEDGMENTS

Emma Exley instigated our professional path by directing us to fun, inspirational places where we found passion and our purpose. Over the years, you have been our model and muse, our sounding board, and creative producer. Naturally, you are our proudest achievement.

There would be no play if not for the projects illustrated in this book, instigated by visionary clients and collaborators: Young At Art Museum; DuPage Children's Museum; the Art Institute of Chicago; The Patricia & Phillip Frost Art Museum; St. Augustine Lighthouse & Maritime Museum; Field Museum; Ronald McDonald House Charities; Lagoon Explora (Brazil); Chicago Children's Museum; Exploration Station; Mid-Michigan Children's Museum; The Latin School of Chicago; St. Chrysostom's Day School; Evanston Public Library; Fountaindale Public Library; Lincoln Park Zoo; Kansas Children's Discovery Center; and the scores of other museum, entertainment, hospitality, civic, healthcare, and residential clients we have worked with since 1994.

To our mentors and early employers, we thank you for the influential and formative experiences we enjoyed: Steven Izenour, Denise Scott Brown, Robert Venturi, and the lifelong friends that were made along with the discovery of work-life balance in the office of Venturi Scott Brown and Associates; and Skidmore Owings & Merrill offices in Boston, Chicago, and London, where we discovered rigor, good habits, and an endless quest for excellence.

Architecture Is Fun would like to thank and acknowledge the collaborators and Architects of Record for the following illustrated projects: EHDD Architecture (Lincoln Park Zoo); Nagle Hartray Architecture (DuPage Children's Museum, The Latin School of Chicago: Interactive Science Forum, Fountaindale Public Library, and Evanston Public Library); Moline Design Group (Exploration Station); Carow Architects Planners (Bonner Heritage Farm); AECOM/Glavovic Studio (Young At Art Museum); Hoerr Schaudt (Lagoon Explora); Arup (Field Museum); and Constantine Vasilios & Associates (Ronald McDonald House).

Thank you to the many architects, storytellers, photographers, designers, scientists, artists, writers, thinkers, and master builders who have worked with our studio over the years. We would like to recognize their essential and enthusiastic contributions: Doug Snower; Matt Wargo; Adrian Ferguson; Shalini Agrawal; Joseph Altshuler; Amy Batchu; Therese Marie Blazek; Miguel Canon; Meredith Corbett; Dana Crawford; Ryan Dalgaard; Juliann Elliott; Michael Genge; Michael Jividen; Chinatsu Kaneko; Adya Kashuba; Eylül Kethüda Wintermeyer; Kelly Lovell; Nicole Miller; Alan Salabert; Mike Turner; Anne Wells Jernigan; Sudie Wentling; Jay Youn; Richard Kasemsarn; Linda Jackson; Norbert Marszalek; Anita Ambriz; Yu Chiu; Thorsten Bösch; Nick Glazebrook;

Matthew Hoffman; Pablo Cano; Leonel Matheu; Steven Haulenbeek; Doug Fogelson; Paul Orselli; Raul Silva; DeLoss McGraw; Edouard Duval-Carrié; Rob Cabrera; Jim Zahn and Werner Sabo; Jeff Smiejek; Morley Exhibits; Chicago Scenic Studios; Superior Exhibits & Design Inc.; and Redbox Workshop.

Fun and guidance come from our colleagues: Mark Dytham; Astrid Klein; Giles and Connie Moore; Scott Rappe and Grace Kuklinski Rappe; Frank Kavanagh; Tom Brock and Kelly Ducheny; Constantine Vasilios and Anna Nowobilski; John Kelly; Tony Hurtig; Charles and Kathryn Shenk; Atticus Hainsworth and Hilda Mulrooney; Zurich Esposito and Brian McCormick; Joan Pomaranc; Mike Waldinger; Dan Vieyra; Brian and Gillian Wall; Chris Lee and Hillary Johnson; Tom Jacobs; Pete Landon and Karen Patinkin; Carolyn Armenta Davis; Dan and Julie Wheeler; Larry Kearns; Doug and Donna Hanson; John Clark; Miguel del Rio; Jeff Flemming; Rik and Peg Master; Tom Zurowski; Walter Street III and Sheila Radford-Hill; Audrey Jonas; Karen Patel; Cathy Ivcich; and Rochelle Baker.

Blair Kamin and Kristen Richards were the first to write about our work. Lara Brown, Ed Keegan, Anjulie Rao, Cindy Coleman, and Joe Boschetti were among many generous writers, journalists, and colleagues who saw fit to put Architecture Is Fun into print. Gratitude to Nicole Boehringer, Georgia (Gina) Tsarouhas, and Images Publishing for collaborating not once, but twice. Dianne Frank—thank you for always elevating our writing to yet another level.

There is a unique camaraderie that exists among architects. For us, the epicenter of this is the American Institute of Architects. The opportunity for Peter to serve and the confidence placed in him being elected as the 97th President of the AIA is a career-defining honor. Working alongside AIA member and staff colleagues on Boards, Strategic Councils, committees, task forces et al is an ongoing master class validating the investment in furthering and upholding our values as architects. Of particular note are colleagues on the AIA Boards during the years 2017–2021.

We have found purpose and direction in the collegial surroundings of Newcastle University, the University of Pennsylvania, and especially at the School of the Art Institute of Chicago. Our classmates, professors, students, fellow faculty, and administrators are an intellectual driving force. Odile Compagnon, Garret Eakin, May Hawfield, Jerry Hausman, Drea Howenstein, Tony Jones, Jaak Jürisson, Linda Keane, Don Kalec, Anders Nereim, Angela Paterakis, John Ploof, Stephanie Slaughter, and Lisa Wainwright are among particularly supportive influences.

The precedents and values set by Sally Ludman, Nathan Ludman, Patricia Exley and John Exley, and siblings Anita, Dianne, and Judith deserve special recognition. We are grateful for their influences and unwavering support.

Chicago, 2021

THE ELEMENTS OF DYNAMIC SYMMETRY
ONE BOMB AWAY
JEAN GEBSER
THE EVER-PRESENT ORIGIN
MIND

FIRM PROFILE

Architecture Is Fun makes everyday life fun. Architecture Is Fun is a collaborative practice that explores the nexus of architecture, education, community, and experience. Spreading our influence as educative design strategists, we are a studio that designs, builds, and consults with our neighbors and with major organizations in a myriad of fields, on a wide range of issues. We are committed to building the accessible places of learning, living, working, play, and fun that we believe are indispensable for human growth and development.

Peter Exley is an established architect with a social agenda. He believes that successful architecture comes about when the dialogue on design involves the entire community. When people make places together, good things happen in play, work, and life. As a social and cultural activist, Peter enjoys working with local and global leaders to envision and build resilient cities through art and architecture, one project at a time.

Peter is the 97th President of the American Institute of Architects, a thought leader, professor, mentor, and lover of architecture, rock 'n' roll music, and Leeds United. He believes that architecture is one of our gateways to a more empathetic and equitable future.

Sharon Exley is a leading educative designer with a singular aesthetic desire; she wants you to discover beauty and play in architecture. Sharon is a culture builder, author, and developer of Architecture Is Fun's philosophy of participatory design. She embraces the intersection of design and pedagogy, visual arts, and arts as visual feasts. Sharon pays it forward by mentoring the next generation of talented women, whom she encourages to be entrepreneurial, adventurous, and to establish work-life balance surrounded by beautiful art, architecture, design, data, education, activism, and collaboration. She is the quintessential finder of fun.

IMAGE CREDITS

Cover illustration by Peter Exley. All diagrams, graphs, illustrations, and maps are by Architecture Is Fun. Photography is courtesy of Architecture Is Fun, with the following exceptions.

© Burpee Museum of Natural History || 170 top

© Kenn Busch || 121

© Children's Museum of Fond du Lac || 175 top

© Doug Fogelson || 188

© Doug Snower Photography || 12, 43 center left, top right, and bottom, 44–47, 49–53, 55–59, 61 top and bottom right, 62–64, 66–67, 68, 69 bottom, 72–75, 76–77, 78, 79 bottom, 80 top right and bottom, 81, 105 top left and bottom, 106–7, 109 bottom right, 110–11, 112 top, 113, 115–17, 119 bottom, 120, 123–25, 127–29, 131–33, 135–39, 141–45, 147–49, 151–53, 160 top, 161 top, 162 bottom, 163, 164, 166–67, 168 top, 169 top, 170 bottom, 171–74, 175 bottom, 176, bottom, 177 bottom, 178 bottom, 179 bottom, 181 bottom, 182–5

© DuPage Children's Museum || 112 bottom

© Emma Exley || 69 top, 160 bottom, 168 bottom

© Peter Exley || 36–37, 90, 92, 165 top

© Sharon Exley || 79 top left and right, 80, 82–83, 97, 101 top right, 105 top right, 109 top and bottom left, 157, 165 bottom, 169 bottom, 177 top, 180 bottom, 181 top

© Florida International University || 85–89, 161 bottom

© Steve Kagan || 162 top

© Jim Lincoln || 180 top

© Matt Wargo Photography || 91, 93–96, 98–99, 101 top left and bottom, 102–3

© Mid-Michigan Children's Museum || 119 top

© RMHC || 43 top left

© Sam Grant Photo || 6

© visualizedconcepts inc., rendering || 176 top, 177 top

© Young At Art Museum || 65, 70–71

Published in Australia in 2021 by
The Images Publishing Group Pty Ltd
ABN 89 059 734 431

Offices

Melbourne
6 Bastow Place
Mulgrave, Victoria 3170
Australia
Tel: +61 3 9561 5544

New York
6 West 18th Street 4B
New York, NY 10011
United States
Tel: +1 212 645 1111

Shanghai
6F, Building C, 838 Guangji Road
Hongkou District, Shanghai 200434
China
Tel: +86 021 31260822

books@imagespublishing.com
www.imagespublishing.com

The Images Publishing Group Reference Number: 1586

NATIONAL LIBRARY OF AUSTRALIA

A catalogue record for this book is available from the National Library of Australia

Title: Architecture Is Fun // Sharon Exley and Peter Exley
ISBN: 9781864708943

This title was commissioned in IMAGES' Melbourne office and produced as follows:
Editorial Georgia (Gina) Tsarouhas, *Art direction/production* Nicole Boehringer

Printed by Artron Art Printing (HK) Limited, on 157gsm Chinese OJI matt art paper

MIX
Paper from responsible sources
FSC® C019910
www.fsc.org

IMAGES has included on its website a page for special notices in relation to this and its other publications. Please visit www.imagespublishing.com